Largest Churches
In The
United States

Compiled
By
Dr. Alton E. Loveless

Compiled
By
Dr. Alton E. Loveless

ISBN 978-1-940609-99-7
Soft cover

This book was printed in the United States of America.

To order additional copies of this book contact:

FWB Publications
Enchanted Acres
1006 Rayme Drive
Columbus, Ohio 43207

FWB

Introduction

The number of megachurches in the United States has grown tremendously over the past 20 years, which suggests this innovative American institution has taken root and is thriving.

In 1990, the United States had one megachurch per 4 million people but by 2005 the terrain had shifted to four megachurches per one million Americans.

Recent studies, by the Hartford Institute for Religion Research and the Dallas-based church resource center Leadership Network, have mapped the dramatic growth of Protestant churches in the United States with a weekly attendance of 2,000 people or more. Many of these churches are located in the South and in the West, and nearly all of them worship in a contemporary style that embraces the latest technology

In nearly all megachurches the senior pastor is a main attraction and is one of the primary draws for new members. Nearly all megachurches use electric guitars and drums, as well as visual projection equipment. Ninety percent of megachurches described their services as spiritually alive, joyful, inspirational, and thought-provoking.

Between 35 and 40 percent of these churches are non-denominational. Many others minimize their denominational ties, most obviously by dropping the affiliation from the church's name. Older megachurches do not look like newer ones and larger ones function differently than smaller ones. Likewise, the race of the pastor makes some difference as does the theological orientation of the church.

In this book I have listed every church I could find that had an attendance of 1000 and above. They represent most states.

I am grateful for denominational lists, websites of these churches, and this work has been a compilation of many sources to bring this book to you.

Table of Contents

Alaska

Anchorage Baptist Temple Anchorage   AK   2200

1956: Missionary Don White established the Bible Baptist Church of Anchorage, Alaska on DeBarr road. He served as pastor for fifteen years, and the church grew to about 325 regular attendees.

1971: Jerry Prevo was called to pastor this church at which time the attendance began to increase rapidly. Pastor Prevo then founded the Anchorage Christian Schools. In just a few short years, the church exceeded the capacity of their existing facilities and needed to do something to allow for further growth.

1973: The church moved to their present location of twenty acres on Northern Lights Boulevard. The new building was primarily built by church members freely volunteering their time and talents. At this time the church was renamed Anchorage Baptist Temple.

1976: A gymnasium and additional classrooms were built to accommodate the growing needs of Anchorage Christian Schools.

1981: A new addition was added to make room for church offices and even more classrooms.

1983: The entire facility became one structure when the building of a multipurpose room connected the gymnasium and the church auditorium.

1988: The church became owner and operator of KCFT Christian Television (Channel 35) proclaiming the Gospel 24 hours a day, seven days a week to over half of the state's population.

1992: A beautiful 2100-seat auditorium was built and the old auditorium was converted into classrooms.

1996: Additional classrooms (27,000 square feet) were built for the Day School and Sunday School programs.

2002: The church completed a 75,000 square feet Children's Ministry Center. This facility consists of 26 classrooms for Sunday School and Anchorage Christian School. It also has a

300-seat gymnasium, library, music department, computer lab, and chemistry lab.

ChangePoint, Anchorage, AK Dan Jarrell, 4,500

ChangePoint's story stretches over 25 years. In 1989 our church body started as a handful of people meeting in South Anchorage. Since then ChangePoint remains a community committed to being transformed by Jesus together.

We are a community of broken people discovering what it means to enjoy God together. We are about being transformed by the person of Jesus. We are committed to demonstrating the heart of Jesus to Alaska and the world beyond. We are about professing redemption, not perfection. We are about making disciples and being disciples.

Ultimately, we are about the gospel woven into our lives and changing who we are, because we are about Jesus.

The best way to truly find out about us is to join us and hear firsthand how the transformational power of Jesus is continually changing us.

Alabama

3Circle Church, Fairhope AL 1,665

Our main gathering times for the Eastern Shore campus are Sunday mornings at 8:00, 9:30, and 11:15. The teaching in all 3 gatherings is identical each week, and we provide exciting ministry for children during all 3, as well.

Our gathering time for our Midtown, Thomasville and Semmes campuses is Sunday mornings at 10:00

We dress very casually at 3Circle Church; all we ask is that you are mindful of dressing modestly.   The church staff typically wear jeans on Sundays.

We provide exciting and interactive ministry for all ages! On Sunday morning you can find a place for children (age's birth – 4th) grade during all main gatherings. Our Connection Team members will direct you to a check-in point for children.

Small groups for 5th-8th grade students are offered during our third gathering at 11:15. Our large group environment for 5th & 6th graders (Mission 56) takes place on Wednesday nights, 6:00-7:30 in the 3Circle Kids room. 7th-12th grade students (3Circle Students) meet on Wednesday nights, 6:30-8:00 in our student building.

We are a multi-denominational congregation with a Southern Baptist heritage.
Asbury United Methodist   Madison   AL   2500

Briarwood Presbyterian Birmingham AL4,100

Briarwood Presbyterian Church is a flagship congregation of the Presbyterian Church in America located in suburban Birmingham, Alabama.

It was formed in 1960 by the Rev. Frank M. Barker, Jr. and has been a conservative evangelical Protestant congregation since its inception. In September 25, 1960 the church was officially organized, and in 1972 the Briarwood Theological Seminary was chartered. The first General Assembly of the Presbyterian Church in America was held in Briarwood church building in December 4, 1973. In 1988 the church moved to the Acton road property. In 1999, Barker retired after serving as the senior pastor for 40 years, and was succeeded by the Rev. Dr. Harry L. Reeder III, the current minister. Founded in a storefront, it later grew to have what was reported to be the largest church budget in Alabama, and opened a $32 million campus in 1988. In 2011 the expansion of youth project was begun. In 2013 the Children's Auditorium was completed, to allow more space to the even growing children's ministries.

Calvary	Tuscaloosa	AL	1,233
Calvary Baptist Church	Dothan	AL	1,077
Calvary Assembly	Decatur	AL	2200

Church of the Highlands Birmingham AL32,550

Pastor Chris Hodges dreamed of planting a church with a simple goal: help people connect with God in a church without letting structures and programs get in the way. With the help of the Dream Team—34 people committed to seeing this dream become a reality—Church of the Highlands began on February 4, 2001. That first Sunday, over 350 attended at the Fine Arts Center of Mountain Brook High School.

Pastor Chris focused on reaching out to the non-churched community, building relationships through small groups meeting throughout the city. The life-giving message of the Gospel, the passion and joy of Sunday Celebrations, and the simple style of Church of the Highlands brought immediate growth. In its first year, the church grew to 600 in weekly attendance, and 371 people committed their lives to Christ. At the same time, the church helped in the planting of six other churches and gave nearly a quarter of its income to missions.

The church established an office complex in March 2002 and established a second identical service that Easter. In its third year, Church of the Highlands had over 1,400 in weekly attendance and more than 1,600 people attending one of their 85 small groups.

As Church of the Highlands is in its second decade, the church has grown to more than 30,000 people attending each weekend with even more participating in over 3,200 small groups. Church of the Highlands offers contemporary, biblically-driven worship services that are alive with energy and creativity, as well as excellent childcare, exciting children's and student ministries, and dynamic small groups.

Christ United Methodist	Mobile	AL	2095
Cove Church Owens	Cross Roads	AL	2000
Crosspoint Southern Baptist	Trussville	AL	1,317
Dawson Memorial Baptist	Homewood	AL	2,875

Dayspring Baptist Church   Mobile   AL   1,190

Daystar Church	Cullman	AL	2000
Decatur Baptist	Decatur	AL	1,039
East Memorial Bapt	Prattville	AL	1,784
First Baptist Church	Enterprise	AL	1,050
Epicchurch.Tv	Decatur	AL	2081
Faith Chapel Chr.	Birmingham	AL	6,400
First Baptist Church	Tuscaloosa	AL	3000
First Baptist Church	Pelham	AL	1,100
First Baptist	Saraland	AL	1,177
First Baptist Church	Montgomery	AL	2500

Frazer United Methodist Montgomery AL **8,000**

In the 1960s, Frazer Memorial Methodist Church had about 500 members. Interstates 85 and 65 were planned to intersect just a few blocks west of the church. This intersection required the purchase of large plots of land near the church building. Most people in the parish area had to relocate to other sections of the city. It became apparent that the interstate system had destroyed the neighborhood concept around which Frazer Memorial was built. Furthermore, relocation of the church property appeared difficult because there was no particular section of the city to which many members had moved. Some denominational consultants studied the problem and basically suggested the church disband and encouraged the members to join Methodist congregations near their new residence.

After more discussion, the pastor, Rev. Noah Lisenby, is reported to have leaped out of his chair, looked at the people present, and said, "You may know statistics and demographics, but you don't know the heart of the people of Frazer, and you don't understand God's purpose for these people!" The people of Frazer felt that God had a plan and a purpose for them.

Eventually, five acres of property in East Montgomery were offered to the church. Again, the people of Frazer were told that relocation would not work because there was not a single member living within three miles of the new property! It was estimated that fewer than 50 percent of the people would relocate. Again, people did not know the heart of the Frazer family. At the time of relocation, Frazer did not lose a single member.

Over the next 30 years, Frazer became one of the fastest growing United Methodist congregations in America. In 1990 it had the largest worship attendance and the largest Sunday School attendance of any United

Methodist congregation in North America!

To reach even more people, Frazer began to offer three Sunday morning worship services and Sunday School hours in 1978. This required much change, but the needs of others proved more important than comfortable routines. In 1992, Frazer invested in a state-of-the-art television ministry and studio to take the message of Christ to the greater Montgomery community, state, nation and even the world.

Since Easter Sunday 2000, Frazer has increased the number of Sunday morning worship services to six by starting three Contemporary Worship services. In 2003, a seventh service, totally in Spanish, was begun and a fulltime Hispanic minister was hired. This service is having a major impact on the growing Hispanic community in our area. These services are incorporating new methods to communicate the timeless truth of Jesus to a new generation.

On July 17, 2005, Frazer opened its newest building, which includes the 2000-seat Wesley Hall, a large atrium, bookstore, coffee shop, baptistery and new Children's Ministry facilities. Wesley Hall is now the new home for our Contemporary Worship services and is ideal for concerts, plays and seasonal musical/drama productions.

Gardendale First Baptist	Gardendale	AL	3,757
Golden Acres Baptist	Phenix City	AL	1,150

Highland Park	Muscle Shoals	AL	1,024
Hill Crest	Anniston	AL	1,375
Hunter Street Baptist	Hoover	AL	2,916
Harvest Church of God	Anniston	AL	2000
Huntsville First Baptist	Huntsville	AL	1,019
Independent Presbyterian	Birmingham	AL	2,400
Kingwood Church	Alabaster	AL	2000
Lakeview	Auburn	AL	1,021
Lindsay Lane Baptist	Athens	AL	1,167
Mayfair Church of Christ	Huntsville	AL	1800
Metro Church of God	Birmingham	AL	2000
Montgomery First	Montgomery	AL	1,958
Mount Zion Baptist	Huntsville	AL	1,219
More Than Conquerors	Birmingham	AL	3000
Mountaintop Community	Birmingham	AL	2000
New Hope Baptist Church	Birmingham	AL	3000
Lindsay Lane Baptist	Athens	AL	1800
Oakwood College Church	Huntsville	AL	2000
Opelika First	Opelika	AL	2,541
Prattville First Baptist	Prattville	AL	1,221
Ridgecrest Baptist Church	Dothan	AL	1,638
Shades Mountain Baptist	Vestavia Hills	AL	2,450
Sixth Avenue Baptist	Birmingham	AL	2000
The Church at Brook Hills	Birmingham	AL	4,133
The Rock Family Worship	Huntsville	AL	4,500
Tillman's Corner First	Mobile	AL	1,055
Tuscaloosa First	Tuscaloosa	AL	1,650
The Worship Center Chr.	Birmingham	AL	2,000
Word Alive International	Oxford	AL	3,300
Valley View	Tuscaloosa	AL	1,040
Westwood Baptist Church	Alabaster	AL	1,305
Whitesburg Baptist	Huntsville	AL	1,709
Willowbrook Baptist	Huntsville	AL	2,845

Arkansas

Benton First Baptist	Benton	AR	1,100
Bentonville First Baptist	Bentonville	AR	1,200
Brand New Church	Harrison	AR	3,000
Central Baptist Church	Marked Tree	AR	2,300
Central Baptist Church	Jonesboro	AR	3,319

Cross Church Springdale AR 8,562

Currently Cross Church has five campuses throughout Northwest Arkansas and Southwest Missouri. In 2001, First Baptist Church of Springdale became a multi-campus ministry with the beginning of The Church at Pinnacle Hills in Rogers. In 2010, the church changed its name to Cross Church, and in 2011, the church further expanded its ministry with the beginning of a campus in the city of Fayetteville. Cross Church was then gifted with College Avenue Baptist Church, also in Fayetteville, and has been meeting there since April 2012. Most recently Cross Church launched its fifth campus on April 20, 2014 in Neosho, MO. Thousands gather in multiple worship venues weekly. While meeting at various local sites and five campuses, the church is committed to planting churches regionally, nationally, and internationally.

| Downtown Church-Christ | Searcy | AR | 2,000 |
| Church of Christ Family | Pine Bluff | AR | 1,750 |

Fellowship Bible Church Little Rock AR 5,000

In the late 1960s a group of students at the University of Arkansas in Fayetteville were inspired with a vision for a new kind of church. This band of friends believed that God had given them a vision for doing something spectacular in the name of Christ. In 1977, the group, with fewer than 30 worshippers began meeting in a home in Little Rock. On August 21 of the same year Fellowship Bible Church held its first official service at Little Rock's Anthony School.

In the 1980's as the church grew, services moved to the Pulaski Academy gymnasium then again to a local movie theatre. In 1985, Fellowship built its own worship center and by the mid-90's five free-standing buildings formed the church. Fellowship's leadership began considering how it could make a greater impact in the communities around the Little Rock area, so in 2004 Fellowship became a multisite church launching its first campus in Benton and just three years later launching another campus in Cabot. Fellowship was now 'one church in many locations.'

In May of 2008 Fellowship moved to its current facilities believing once again God had provided for our needs as a growing congregation. Over the years Fellowship has been involved in ministries around Arkansas and throughout the world. We have been used by God to plant churches, partner with other ministries across the globe, send and support missionaries, and provide resources for outreach and discipleship. The means and methods of ministry may have changed over the years but our passion and vision have remained the same and burns as bright as it ever has. We want to be a people of God who make disciples who live by His grace and for His glory at home and across the World!

Fellowship Bible Church Rogers AR 8,000

Late in the fall of 1983, seven families from four different churches met together. One particular concern united them on that evening of careful consideration. The question addressed was simple, yet also complex: "Was there a need in the Northwest Arkansas area for a new church with a distinctive emphasis and approach to ministry?" After discussion and prayer, the families were unanimous; there definitely was a need for such a church. On December 8, 1983, the seven couples met and committed to spend seven days in prayer concerning two questions. First, were they willing to become part of a new church? Second, would they be willing to sacrificially give of their time, resources and skills to help the church get started?

The following Sunday, the families came together and voted unanimously to begin Fellowship Bible Church of Northwest Arkansas. Effective February 1, 1984, the first pastor (Dr. Robert Cupp) of Fellowship Bible Church began a part-time ministry with the new church. Beginning February 5, the church family met each Sunday in the Benton County Public Services Building. Throughout the spring, several families joined the core of the new church.

When Fellowship officially opened to the public on Sunday, May 27, 1984, the core of the church had grown to seventeen.

For three years (1984-1987), Fellowship Bible met in the rented facilities of the Seventh Day Adventist Church. In June of 1987, the growing congregation moved to Oakdale Junior High in Rogers. For four years (1987-1991), this school was the Sunday home of Fellowship Bible Church of Northwest Arkansas. The church began to take on a decidedly "regional" complexion. On June 16, 1991, Fellowship dedicated its first building on Pleasant Grove Road. Fellowship has expanded the current campus several times since the initial building was erected.

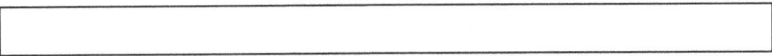

Fellowship implemented the multi-congregational approach to ministry in September of 1998 with the addition of our Saturday Night congregation (now called "Mosaic"). Since then, several other congregations have either formed at

Fellowship or developed a close partnership with Fellowship. The Grove Church, Samaritan House Fellowship, White River Fellowship, New Heights Church, The Church at Springdale, Grace Church, Celebrate Recovery, and others have all been ministry partners of the original church body.

Fellowship has embraced the concept of team staffing. We use teams to teach, lead worship, do student ministry, children's ministry and just about any other ministry we have engaged. The staff team, under the leadership of the Elder Board, exists to serve the greater team of our lay leaders. The staff team is here to equip and enable them to do ministry. (Ephesians 4:11-12) We want to produce and release spiritual leaders.

The staff team concept also keeps Fellowship from becoming a personality-driven church. This is Christ's church and we are here to serve him. We often say around Fellowship, "We want our name nowhere and our influence everywhere." This is not only true of our church, but also of our staff. Our staff ministers are to be humble servants.

Fellowship Bible Church	Little Rock	AR	4000
Fellowship Bible Church	Benton	AR	6000
Fellowship Bible Church	Lowell	AR	7,000
First Assembly of God	N Little Rock	AR	3,300
First Baptist Church	Bentonville	AR	2,200
First Baptist Church	Jonesboro	AR	2,000
First Baptist Church	Fort Smith	AR	1,414
Geyer Springs First Bapt.	Little Rock	AR	2,118

Harvest Time	Fort Smith	AR	2,200
First Baptist Church	Hot Springs	AR	1,042
Immanuel Baptist Church	Little Rock	AR	1,300

New Life Church Conway AR 8,205

New life story began with a god-breathed calling to reach the state of Arkansas. We made the move from Louisiana with our four young children in November of 2000. On February 4, 2001, we had our first service in a renovated car dealership in downtown Conway with a handful of committed people who were willing to serve. By the unexplainable grace of God, NLC has grown far beyond what any of us could have imagined in those first few days.

In August 2001, we opened our second campus in Maumelle. Over the following year, that campus began to grow exponentially as people invested in the vision. From the outset of this journey, we have been grateful to work long side an incredible team of pastors and leaders in each city who help carry out the vision God placed in our hearts.

Rogers First   Rogers   AR   1,835

Russellville First Baptist   Russellville   AR 1,050

Saint Mark Baptist Church Little Rock AR 8,000

With only four members, Saint Mark Baptist Church was founded in 1892 in a nameless storehouse in downtown Little Rock. Through our obedience to God's divine direction and guidance, Saint Mark has flourished and is impacting our community in awesome ways.

From small group lessons to help our members learn how to better manage their finances, to our food programs for the homeless, disaster relief assistance, and educational tutoring for our youth, Saint Mark uses biblical principles to help our families grow in every aspect of their lives.

We have grown to a ministry that includes nearly 9,000 members, three Sunday services, three Wednesday services, a broadcast television ministry and a robust community outreach ministry.

The Church at Rock Creek   Little Rock   AR   4,500

**The growth of the churches
in this book
are moving and reaches
greatly in the areas where they are
located.**

Arizona

Calvary Baptist Church   Lake Havasu City AZ 1,086
Calvary Chapel   Tucson   AZ 8,000

Calvary Community Church Phoenix AZ 11,433

Calvary Community Church is known for a love of God's Word and celebration of His Grace toward us. One reason these qualities are so strong at Calvary goes back to our beginning in 1982 when Pastor J. Mark Martin left a legalistic, unbiblical denomination because he was compelled to teach the Good News of God's love and salvation by faith in Jesus. Calvary, a non-denominational church, started with only 11 people in a northwest Phoenix elementary school band room and today has grown to be the church home for over 12,000 believers. You will love Pastor Mark's dedication to the Word and how he brings the Bible alive in a way you can understand and enjoy. You can view or listen to a recent message online at our **Media**

Library. We meet at two campus locations: a former shopping center right off the Black Canyon Freeway near Cactus, and also at a former theater located at 59th Avenue and Bell. Your kids will love our extensive and well-staffed Children's Ministries, some of the best you'll find anywhere.

Casas Adobes Baptist Church   Tucson AZ   1,812
Central Christian Church   Mesa   AZ   8,786

Christ's Church of the Valley Peoria AZ 20,000

Christ's Church of the Valley is a non-denominational Christian megachurch located in Peoria, Arizona, currently with other locations in Surprise, Scottsdale, Anthem and Mesa. The church was founded in 1982 by senior pastor Dr. Donald Wilson. Weekend church attendance exceeds 25,000,[1] making it the largest non-denominational church in Arizona and the 6th largest church in the United States. The church currently employs over 200 full-time and part-time staff members.

| Mission Community Church | Gilbert | AZ 6,000 |
| North Phoenix Baptist Church | Phoenix | AZ 1,600 |

Phoenix First Assembly of God Phoenix AZ 21,000

Phoenix First is an Assemblies of God megachurch in Phoenix, Arizona. As of 2011, it was one of the largest Assembly of God churches in the U.S. with an average weekly attendance of 10,000.

Its largest events every year include Pastors School, in which thousands of pastors and workers come from all over the country to learn from Pastor Tommy Barnett how to make a church grow. Another notable event is The Great Turkey Giveaway. This event occurs around Thanksgiving and provides some 3,000 turkeys for underprivileged families that the church busses in from all over Phoenix. Yet another event is the Great Toy Giveaway. This occurs around Christmas and the church gives away over 10,000 presents to Phoenix's underprivileged children.

Other notable achievements of First Assembly include The Los Angeles Dream Center, The Phoenix Dream Center and The New York City Dream Center. These are rehabilitation centers that take in the homeless for free and provide them with the means to overcome addiction, abuse, and an assortment of other burdens people pick up in life. The Los Angeles Dream Center is run by Matthew Barnett, Tommy Barnett's son.

It has an indoor stadium-like sanctuary that seats 7,000 people. It has 2nd- and 3rd-level balconies on most of the circumference of the auditorium. The church also features an elevator, cafe and a bookstore.

Scottsdale Bible Church   Scottsdale AZ 6,234
The Living Word Bible Church   Mesa   AZ 7,500

California

Abundant Life Christian	Mountain View	CA	4,500
Acts Full Gospel Church	Oakland	CA	6,000
Angelus Temple	Los Angeles	CA	8,300
Antioch Church	Long Beach	CA	1,200
Bay Area Christian Church	Palo Alto	CA	3,600

Bayside Covenant Church Roseville CA 11,327
Bayside Church is a mega church located in the Citrus Heights area in Roseville, CA. Bayside Church, formally known as Bayside Covenant Church, is a family of churches and venues centered on its primary campus in Roseville, California, USA, which is referred to as the Granite Bay campus. The Church is led by Senior Pastor Ray Johnston, Teaching Pastors Curt Harlow and Andrew McCourt, and Worship Pastor Lincoln Brewster. John Jackson, the former executive pastor at Bayside, became the president of William Jessup University on March 23, 2011. Bayside is one of the largest churches in the Sacramento metropolitan area. It is affiliated with the Evangelical Covenant Church.

On January 1, 2005, Bayside Church planted Bayside of South Sacramento (BOSS) on the southern side of Sacramento. Sherwood Carthen, the chaplain of the Sacramento Kings, was chosen to head the church. The church's membership grew to 330 people within a month, meeting at Luther Burbank High School. BOSS was the first of several church plants planned by the Granite Bay campus.

Between April and May 2010, the church hosted an exhibit including portions of the Dead Sea Scrolls that were obtained by Azusa Pacific University in 2009, as well as historical Bibles and other Christian works.

Bayside hosted over one thousand worship leaders, musicians, songwriters, pastors, technicians, and artists at the Thriving Musician Summit in mid-September 2010. The church featured artists Matt Redman, Paul Baloche, Lincoln Brewster, and Phil Keaggy.

Bayside hosts an annual Thrive Leadership Conference every year where 3,000 pastors and church leaders from many cities come to worship, hear from speakers and be inspired by Bayside volunteers.

As of spring 2015, attendance has grown to over 14,000, with eight church services every weekend at the Granite Bay campus, a Sunday service at both the Folsom and Blue Oaks campuses, and three Sunday services at the Midtown Sacramento campus, Each Bayside campus has its own pastor and worship team.

Bel Air Presbyterian	Los Angeles	CA	3,800
Berendo Street Baptist	Los Angeles	CA	1,800
Bethel Church	San Jose	CA	2,200
Bethel Church	Redding	CA	3,500
Bethel Korean Church	Irvine	CA	5,000
Big Valley Grace Comm.	Modesto	CA	5,000
Calvary Chapel Chino Valley	Chino	CA	8,500
Calvary Chapel	Costa Mesa	CA	9,500
Calvary Chapel	Downey	CA	7,000

Calvary Chapel Diamond Bar CA 12,000

Raul Ries is the Senior Pastor of Calvary Chapel Golden Springs and President of Somebody Loves You Ministries.

After his miraculous conversion in 1972, Raul began to read and study the Bible extensively, regardless of his former poor study habits in high school. In 1974, he began a home Bible study with seven other committed individuals. He started to preach and counsel the youth during the noon hour at his former high school, Baldwin Park High. Soon after, Raul would visit several high school campuses each week conducting Bible studies.

Calvary Chapel West Covina grew out of Raul's home fellowship. As the fellowship grew, it moved to his Kung-Fu studio, then to the Fox Theatre and was soon meeting weekly at a converted Safeway store in 1979 with 800 people.

In 1993, the congregation moved to Diamond Bar, into a 101,000 square-foot corporate building on twenty-eight acres. Calvary Chapel Golden Springs (as it is now known) draws between 12,000 and 14,000 in attendance weekly.

Somebody Loves You Ministries, directed by Raul Ries, encompasses radio broadcasts, concert evangelism, concert outreaches, book publishing and film/video production.

Raul Ries is heard internationally on more than 350 radio stations and translators on the daily 30-minute syndicated radio program, Somebody Loves You.

Over the years, Ries' outreaches, from the Exit Festivals in the United States and the Escape Festivals in South America to the Somebody Loves You Concerts around the world, have seen thousands of men, women and children in attendance, with many making decisions for Christ. The high-energy concerts feature popular Christian rock and alternative bands with a simple and straightforward message by Raul Ries. While attracting all ages, the concerts have a high percentage of youth in attendance.

His great love for the Word made him pursue higher education and he now holds three Master Degrees from Azusa Pacific University and a Doctor of Ministry from Fuller Theological Seminary.

Calvary Chapel	Gardena	CA	9,000
Calvary Chapel	San Jose	CA	7,800
Church Good Shepherd	San Diego	CA	7,500
City of Refuge	Gardena	CA	10,000
Clovis Hills Community	Clovis	CA	1,248
Cornerstone Church	National City	CA	6,300
Crossroads Christian	Corona	CA	8,375
Eastside Christian Church	Anaheim	CA	4,400
Emmanuel Presbyterian	San Jose	CA	2,500
Faithful Central MissBapt	Inglewood	CA	7,250
Family Community	San Jose	CA	3,365

First African Methodist Episcopal
Los Angeles CA 10,000

The First African Methodist Episcopal Church of Los Angeles (First A.M.E. or FAME) is a megachurch in Los Angeles, California, part of the African Methodist Episcopal (AME) Church. It is the oldest church founded by African Americans in Los Angeles, dating to 1872. The church now has a membership of more than 19,000 individuals.

First Chinese Baptist   Los Angeles   CA 1,700
First Chinese Baptist   Walnut   CA 1,005
First Evangelical Free   Fullerton   CA 6,000
Friends Church   Yorba Linda   CA 4,000

Glide Memorial Church San Francisco CA 12,750

Glide Memorial Church is a church in San Francisco, California, affiliated with the United Methodist Church, which opened in 1930. Although conservative until the 1960s, since then it has served as a counter-culture rallying point and has been one of the most prominently liberal churches in the United States. Glide is also famous for its Gospel Choir and numerous social service programs.

Since the 1960s, Glide Church has provided various services for the poor and disenfranchised. Glide currently runs 87 various social service programs. Through their Daily Free Meals program, Glide serves three meals daily, amounting to over 750,000 free meals a year.

In 2007, Glide provided 750,000 meals per year through their community clinic, which serves more than 3,000 homeless people. They provided over 100,000 hours of licensed childcare and quality after-school programming to over 325 clients in 2007. They provided emergency supplies to 2,190 individuals in 2006. And they booked 5,707 shelter beds and helped 120 homeless persons move into permanent housing in 2007. According to their website, Glide's daily Free Meals program served 934,000 meals in 2009.

The church also provides HIV testing, mental and primary health care, women's programs, crisis intervention, an after-school program, creative arts and mentoring for youth, literacy classes, computer training, job skills training, drug and alcohol recovery programs, free legal services for the homeless, housing with case management, and much more.

Largely through the actions of its long-time Pastor Cecil Williams, Glide has become known for its often-controversial views on issues such as same sex marriage. Since Williams became Pastor in 1963, Glide has been called the best-known pulpit in Northern California. Some of Williams' controversial actions have included:

- Performing Same-Sex Marriages very early on, even though the United Methodist Church was far from sanctioning them. The United Methodist Church, the Protestant denomination of Christianity with which Glide is affiliated, currently does not allow its Ministers to perform Same-Sex Marriages.

- Removing the Cross inside the Sanctuary at Glide.
- Helping form the Council on Religion and Homosexuality in 1964
- Accepting City subsidies for Glide's charitable work. Seen by some critics as a violation of the separation of Church and State, Glide first started receiving city subsidies for its meals program in 1981. The individual contributions that flow into Glide on Sundays account for a small portion of the budget— less than $640,000 of the foundation's $8.5 million in revenue during 2002, the most recent year for which a financial audit was available Glide also obtains funding from other various fundraising activities such as their Annual Holiday Festival

Grace Community Church Sun Valley CA 9,300

On July 1, 1956, Grace Community Church of the Valley conducted its first public services. Founded as a nondenominational church, its emphasis was on the basics of Christianity. The fledgling church called Dr. Don Householder, one of the great preachers of his generation, to be its founding pastor. Worship services were conducted in the two main rooms of the converted town house, where a wall had been taken down to enable Dr. Householder to see his entire congregation while preaching.

In 1957, services were moved to the newly built chapel at the present location on Roscoe Boulevard. Less than two years later, two services were being conducted on Sunday mornings, the first education building was built to house Sunday school classes, and Grace Church became known as "the fastest growing church in Los Angeles."

Dr. Householder died in April 1965, and in 1966, Dr. Richard Elvee was called to be pastor. Dr. Elvee had become known as a church builder. Grace Church continued to grow under Dr. Elvee's leadership until he passed away in September 1968.

John MacArthur assumed the pastorate of Grace in February 1969. Prior to this, John had been assistant pastor in the church his father led in Burbank; he had also traveled widely as a conference speaker and representative for Talbot Theological Seminary, from which he graduated with honors.

During those early days of John's ministry, the church doubled in size every two years. We moved from meeting in the Chapel to the newly built Family Center (now the Gymnasium) in 1971, and from there into the current Worship Center in 1977. Since then, additional buildings for teaching and fellowship use have been erected, filling a campus that never sleeps. Truly, the Lord has blessed us with exceptional growth in terms of both people and ministries.

More important than numbers, programs, and structures, however, is the foundation for the spiritual life of Grace Community Church that has been built. This foundation includes sound doctrine, spiritual leadership, and active service. We are convinced that God's legacy of faithfulness to us will continue in the future if we remain faithful to Him and His Word.

Harvest Christian Fellowship Riverside CA 15,000

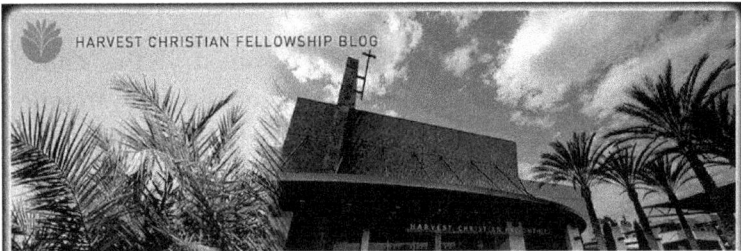

Harvest Christian Fellowship was founded in 1979 by Greg Laurie in Riverside, CA. Laurie has been the senior pastor since that time. Harvest is a megachurch with a congregation of 15,000 and growing. The eighth largest church in America and third largest in California, with satellite campuses in Eastvale (Corona, CA) and Orangecrest (Riverside, CA) and a dedicated campus in Orange County (Irvine, CA). As well as being the launching pad for the International Harvest Crusades, Harvest is involved in other various internal and external ministries.

The vision at Harvest Christian Fellowship is "Knowing God and Making Him Known." While being heavily evangelistic, Greg Laurie also preaches three Sunday morning services at 8:00 am, 10:00 am and 12:00 pm. A fourth service is also held at 6:00 pm and is entitled Sunday nights more by Greg Laurie. Harvest also offers a mid-week study every Wednesday led by Pastor Jeff Lasseigne along with separate High School and Jr. High services. All Sunday and mid-week services are available as a live webcast and are archived for later viewing.

High Desert Church	Victorville	CA	6,313
Horizon Christian Fellowship	San Diego	CA	6,000
Immanuel Baptist Church	Highland	CA	2,543

Jubilee Christian Center San Jose CA 14,000

Jubilee Christian Center, founded by Pastors Dick and Carla Bernal in 1980, is a non-denominational, charismatic church located in the heart of Silicon Valley with a congregation that's celebrated for its varied nationalities and backgrounds.

Jubilee is a large church featuring a variety of ministries that cater to many individual needs, yet it retains the intimacy of a small church. We invite people to "come as you are and let God do the rest."

Our pastors are known worldwide for their compassion and drive. We support Bay Area missions and have a huge presence around the globe – including the remotest spots in India, the Philippines, Africa, Mexico, Haiti, and Panama

– and strive to spread the gospel to as many unchurched people as possible.

Jubilee's Outreach Pantry serves food and household supplies to more than 1,000 families weekly and sponsors annual Backpack, Thanksgiving Dinner, and Christmas Toy Giveaways.

Jubilee's Wednesday, Friday, and Sunday services are live-streamed and thousands of faithful followers around the world tune in to see our weekly messages.

La Familia de Dios	Ontario	CA	2,450
Little Country Church	Redding	CA	3,700
Loma Linda University	Loma Linda	CA	7,000
Magnolia Avenue Baptist	Riverside	CA	1,009
Mandarin Baptist Church	Alhambra	CA	1,698
Maranatha Chapel	San Diego	CA	7,000
Mariners Church	Irvine	CA	13,567
Mosaic LA	Los Angeles	CA	3,570
Mt Calvary Baptist Church	Fairfield	CA	1,700
Neighborhood Church	Redding	CA	2,500
New Life Center	Bakersfield	CA	6,500
New Venture Christian	Oceanside	CA	5,550
New Vision Church	Milpitas	CA	2,300
Newport Church	Newport Beach	CA	5,000
North Coast Calvary Chapel	Carlsbad	CA	6,020

North Coast Church Vista CA 10,000

North Coast Church is a megachurch located in Vista, California, roughly 30 miles north of San Diego. The church also has satellite ("video venue") campuses located in the cities of Carlsbad, Fallbrook and Escondido. It is the largest church in the Evangelical Free Church of America denomination, with about 11,000 people in weekend attendance. In 2006 it was ranked #10 on a list of the "50 most influential churches in America." North Coast has two primary teaching pastors: Larry Osborne and Chris Brown. Larry Osborne has served as a Sr. Pastor and teaching pastor since 1980 while Chris Brown has served as a Sr Pastor and teaching pastor since 2004.

North Valley Baptist Santa Clara CA 3,000

North Valley Baptist Church was established in 1975 with a small band of 75 people. In 1976, Dr. Jack Trieber was called to pastor this infant work. God has greatly blessed the ministry of our pastor. From 1975 to present, more than 2.9 million people have come to hear the preaching of God's Word, with over 62,000 making a profession of faith in Christ for salvation in one of our services, and over 15,000 following the Lord in believer's baptism.

In these last 35 years, God has enabled the church to experience numerous building projects and expand its facilities to include a 65,000-square-foot building at Clyde Avenue, as well as a six-acre college and church campus at De La Cruz Boulevard.

The church reaches out to Santa Clara County through a thriving bus ministry which has brought more than one million people to church over the past thirty-five years. More than one hundred Sunday school classes are available for people of all ages to learn and grow in God's Word. The church's worldwide missions program currently supports about two hundred home and foreign missionaries each month. In addition, there are ministries to numerous non-English-speaking groups, as well as ministries to the deaf, mentally handicapped, a nearby retirement home, and a convalescent hospital.

NorthPointe Community	Fresno	CA	1,986
Onnuri Church Lake View	Terrace	CA	4,500
Paradise Alliance Church	Paradise	CA	2,100
Pathways Community	Santee	CA	1,165
River of Life Christian	Santa Clara	CA	2,950
Rock Harbor Church	Costa Mesa	CA	5,000
Rolling Hills Christian	El Dorado Hills	CA	2,200

Russian Baptist Church West Sacramento CA 2,500

Saddleback Church Lake Forest, California 22,418

Saddleback Church, in Southern California's Orange County, is affiliated with the Southern Baptist Convention. Founded in 1980 by Rick Warren, the church is one of the most prominent evangelical bodies in the nation, and Warren is best known as the author of the 2002 devotional book *The Purpose-Driven Life.*

Sandals Church   Riverside   CA   3,000

Sarang Community Church Anaheim CA 8000

Sarang is a Presbyterian Church in America (PCA) Korean-American church located in Anaheim, California. Sarang has more than 10,000 church attenders. Some statistics estimate about 11,000 members. It is the largest Korean church outside of Korea (Republic of), as well as the largest Asian church outside Asia. In addition, Sarang is the largest congregation within the Presbyterian Church in America.

Sa-Rang Community Church was founded in 1988 by Rev. Oh Jung-hyun.

In 2003 Pastor Oh accepted his call to a megachurch in Seoul Korea of the same name, Sarang Church. In 2004, Rev. SeungWook Kim (Daniel Kim) was called and installed as the new pastor.

In 2011, Pastor Kim accepted his call to pastor a church in Korea called Hallelujah Community Church. In 2012, Rev. ChangSoo Roh was called and installed as the new pastor.

Set Free Christian	Buena Park	CA	6,000
Shadow Mountain Com.	El Cajon	CA	7,513
Shepherd of the Hills	Porter Ranch	CA	8,675
Shiloh Church	Oakland	CA	4,500
Skyline Church	La Mesa	CA	2,500
South Bay Church	San Jose	CA	1,445
Southwinds Church	Tracy	CA	1,113
Spring Hills Community	Santa Rosa	CA	1,300
St. Andrews Presbyterian	Newport Beach	CA	2,000
Sunrise Church	Rialto	CA	6,830
Temple Missionary Bapt.	San Bernardino	CA	1,644
The Church on the Way	Van Nuys	CA	5,000
The Grove Community	Riverside	CA	2,438
The Rock Church	San Diego	CA	12,864
The Rock Church	San Bernardino	CA	9,000
Twin Cities Community	Grass Valley	CA	1,536
Valley Baptist Church	Bakersfield	CA	4,300
Valley Bible Fellowship	Bakersfield	CA	10,300
Venture Christian Church	Los Gatos	CA	3,600

West Angeles Cathedral Los Angeles CA 20,000

West Angeles Church of God in Christ is a Pentecostal Christian church and a member of the Church of God in Christ denomination. Its main place of worship, the *West Angeles Cathedral*, is located in the West Adams Historic District of Los Angeles, California.

It was founded by Elder Clarence E. Church in 1943. The first sanctuary was located on Adams Boulevard, near Interstate 10 (known locally as the Santa Monica Freeway). In 1969 after Elder Church's death, Charles E. Blake, a son of a

pastor and a native of Little Rock, Arkansas, took over as the pastor of West Angeles and has continued to serve as its leader.

Under Blake's leadership, the church has grown from 40 members to over 24,000. The sanctuary has moved twice, first to a 1,000-seat facility (today called the North Campus) located at 3045 Crenshaw Boulevard, and then to the present structure, the 5,000-seat West Angeles Cathedral at 3600 Crenshaw Boulevard. The Cathedral, built from steel, granite and stained glass, was dedicated in 1999. est A" is known for both its influential pastor, dynamic city ministries and for its celebrity members, which include Magic Johnson, Denzel Washington, Stevie Wonder, Michelle Shocked, and Angela Bassett.

WestGate Church   San Jose CA   2,100

Young Nak Presbyterian Los Angeles CA 6,000

Young Nak is a Christian congregation serving the Los Angeles community and seeking, engaging, and encouraging others through a life-changing Christian journey.

Young Nak seeks to be a loving, friendly community that worships God, and serves others. We place a high priority on teaching from the Bible and following the example of Jesus.

Our vision is to impact and renew Los Angeles, California and beyond with the transforming message of Jesus Christ through words and actions.

Colorado

Faith Bible Chapel   Arvada   CO   5,500
Fellowship of The Rockies   Pueblo   CO   1,643

Flatirons Community Church Lafayette CO 15,495

One church three campuses. Our Lafayette Campus is our first location, located in the heart of Lafayette, Colorado. It is our largest location and home to the church offices.

The West Campus, which opened in early 2014 is located right off I-70 in Genesee, Colorado, it's 15 minutes away from towns like Lakewood, Golden, and Evergreen.

The Downtown Campus is located at the intersection of Glenarm Pl. and the 16th Street Mall in downtown Denver.

New Life Church Colorado Springs CO 8,000

New Life Church is a non-denominational charismatic Evangelical Christian megachurch located in Colorado Springs, Colorado, United States. New Life Church has more than 10,000 members. The church was founded by Ted Haggard and is currently pastored by Brady Boyd.

The church established its present campus location in the early 1990s and added buildings and added onto existing buildings in this location. The initial sanctuary on the campus, now referred to as the "theater," seats 1,500 and is used primarily for children's church and youth meetings throughout the week. The current main sanctuary can seat over 8000 but is currently set up to seat 5000.

The New Life campus is also home to the World Prayer Center. The World Prayer Center, through the use of Internet technologies and The World Prayer Team organization, coordinates global prayer efforts among its participants. The World Prayer Center is home to several ministries and internship programs including the Furnace, Burn Student Internship, and the Desperation Leadership Academy.

Riverside Baptist	Denver	CO	2,800
Rocky Mtn Calvary	Colorado Springs	CO	2,000
Timberline Church	Fort Collins	CO	6,022
Village Seven Presbyterian	Colorado Springs	CO	2,100

District of Columbia

Greater Mount Calvary	Washington	DC	7,000
Metropolitan Baptist	Washington	DC	6,000
National Presbyterian	Washington	DC	3,000

Temple of Praise Washington DC 18,000

The Temple of Praise, for decades known as Johenning Baptist Church, was founded in 1916. The legacy began when the Southern Baptist Convention established a training and missionary center to meet the varied needs in a very racially segregated section of southeast, currently known as Washington Highlands/Bellevue. Anna Johenning, a community resident and thrift store owner, initiated many of the missionary activities and the missionary center was ultimately named in her honor. In 1960, as the missionary activities expanded in the growing community, and in response to a call for a more spiritual base for the outreach work, the Baptist Convention built an addition to the missionary center to house church worship services for the predominately white community. As the African American population of Southeast Washington grew, the two congregations separated and the Wayside Chapel was established to sponsor afternoon services for African Americans. In 1969, the chapel was organized as a church, adopting the name Johenning Baptist Church. Sunday, September 2, 1991, Bishop Glen A. Staples, of Beckley, West Virginia, was installed as the third pastor. With the anointing on the life of the new spiritual leader, the former Johenning Baptist Church was a simply a spiritual flower waiting to bloom. In 1993, Bishop Staples revealed a spiritual vision for Johenning that included a new sanctuary and a myriad of community development projects. To that end, Bishop Staples started a mortgage retirement program/building fund. The burning of the church mortgage in October 1998 signaled a commitment to the new vision, a spiritually inspired quest. In November 1998 Johenning purchased the land for a new church home, located just three blocks away. The Johenning Baptist Church changed to an interdenominational worship format and thereby changed its name to the Johenning Temple of Praise. On Easter Sunday, 2004, the first services were held at the new 2,500 seat sanctuary at 700 Southern Avenue, SE. With a new building, and thus a new Christian identity, Johenning became simply the Temple of Praise Church. Bishop Staples, a great visionary, true shepherd, anointed preacher, teacher, and prophet has increased the flock of the church seventy-five fold. Membership has grown from two hundred, in 1991, to over fifteen thousand currently.

Florida

Aloma Church Ministries	Winter Park	FL	1,120
Anastasia Baptist Church	St. Augustine	FL	1,503
Antioch Missionary Baptist	Miami Gardens	FL	7,000
Bay Life Church	Brandon	FL	2,151
Bell Shoals Baptist Church	Brandon	FL	3,593
Bethel Baptist Institutional	Jacksonville	FL	8,000
Calvary Baptist Church	Clearwater	FL	3,478

Calvary Chapel Fort Lauderdale, Florida 18,521

The biggest megachurch in Florida has been going strong for 25 years under the direction of Bob Coy. In addition to a thriving variety of small groups for people of all ages, the church's site archives worship services for streaming or download.

Calvary Chapel	W Melbourne	FL	10,000
Campus Church	Pensacola	FL	7,000
Celebration Church	Jacksonville	FL	11,096
Chets Creek Church	Jacksonville	FL	1,963
Christ Fellowship	Palm Beach Gardens	FL	18,965
Christ Fellowship Baptist	Palmetto Bay	FL	8,197
Christ Life Center	Miami	FL	4,000
Christ's Church	Jacksonville	FL	4,200
Church by the Glades	Coral Springs	FL	7,749
City Church	Tallahassee	FL	1,512
Coral Ridge Presby.	Fort Lauderdale	FL	2,000
Cornerstone Family	St. Cloud	FL	1,042
East Brent Baptist	Pensacola	FL	2,000
El Rey Jesús	Miami	FL	12,540
First Assembly-God	Fort Myers	FL	7,462
First Baptist-the Mall	Lakeland	FL	2,966
First Baptist Church	Brandon	FL	2,875
First Baptist Church	Orlando	FL	1,204

First Baptist Church Jacksonville FL 28,000

First Baptist Church has 28,000 members and an average attendance of around 7,500 for Sunday services, making it the third largest church in the Southern Baptist Convention. The main Downtown Campus comprises nine square blocks of property connected by above-ground crosswalks. The campus includes several auditoriums for services, a Sunday school building, and facilities for First Baptist Academy, a private K-8 school.

First Baptist Church has its origins in the oldest Baptist congregation in Jacksonville, Bethel Baptist Church, established in 1838. The church experienced a period of considerable growth in the mid-20th century, and now encompasses eleven square blocks of downtown Jacksonville. Several former pastors, including Homer G. Lindsay, Jr. and Jerry Vines, were widely influential in the Southern Baptist Convention, leading it in both growth and a shift towards conservatism.

First Baptist Church of Jacksonville has two satellite campuses. Their South Campus meets in the Ponte Vedra High School auditorium in St. Johns County. They recently purchased land in the Nocatee community and will build a full campus on the land. In 2013, the Ortega Campus was opened after FBC JAX acquired Ortega Baptist Church.

First Baptist Church	Kissimmee	FL	1,415
First Baptist	Leesburg	FL	1,081
First Baptist Church	Merritt Island	FL	1,127
First Baptist Church	Middleburg	FL	1,340
First Baptist Church	Naples	FL	3,477
First Baptist Church	Oviedo	FL	2,299
First Baptist Church	Plant City	FL	1,400
First Baptist Church	Umatilla	FL	1,000
First Baptist Church	Weston	FL	1,052
First Baptist Church	Orlando	FL	5,690
First Baptist Church	Windermere	FL	1,454
FishHawk Fellowship	Lithia	FL	1,263
Flamingo Road Baptist	Cooper City	FL	8,500
First Baptist Church	Fort Lauderdale	FL	2,150
Free Life Chapel	Lakeland	FL	2,000
Fruit Cove Baptist Church	Jacksonville	FL	1,222
Grace Family Church	Cheval	FL	6,187
Grace Fellowship	WPalm Beach	FL	2,430
Gulf to Lake Baptist	Crystal River	FL	1,050
Hibernia Baptist Church	Fleming Island	FL	1,400
Hiland Park Baptist Church	Panama City	FL	1,320
Hillcrest Church	Pensacola	FL	1,950
Hopeful Baptist Church	Lake City	FL	1,325

Idlewild Baptist Church	Lutz	FL	6,150
Iglesia Cristiana Segadores de Vida	Hollywood	FL	7,100
Immanuel Baptist Church	Tallahassee	FL	1,127
Indian Rocks First Bapt.	Largo	FL	2,780
Lifepoint Church	Tampa	FL	1,900
McGregor Baptist Church	Fort Myers	FL	2,636
North Jacksonville Baptist	Jacksonville	FL	1,700
Northcliffe Baptist Church	Spring Hill	FL	1,027
Northland, A Church Distributed	Longwood	FL	15,800
Oasis Church of South Florida	Pembroke Pines	FL	2,500
Olive Baptist Church	Pensacola	FL	2,932
Panama City First	Panama City	FL	1,898

Potential Church Fort Lauderdale FL 12,382

Potential Church is a fast-growing, multi-site church running passionately after a huge vision. Currently with six campuses, Potential Church has locations in Cooper City, Hallandale Beach, Miami, and Pensacola, FL as well as Lima, Peru and on the Internet. Under the leadership of Pastor Troy Gramling, Potential Church partners with people to reach their God potential as they connect with God, become like Christ, and influence their world.

Southern Baptist

Church	City	State	Attendance
ReThink Life Church	Orlando	FL	1,000
Russell Miss. Baptist	Green Cove Sps	FL	1,200
Shiloh Metropolitan Baptist	Jacksonville	FL	2,300
South Biscayne Church	North Port	FL	1,296
South Tampa Fellowship	Tampa	FL	1,290
Spanish River Church	Boca Raton	FL	2,000
Summit Church	Fort Myers	FL	2,180
First Baptist Church	Temple Terrace	FL	1,034
The Bridge at Palma Sola Bay	Bradenton	FL	1,000
The Church at Viera	Melbourne	FL	1,087
The Crossing Church	Tampa	FL	4,613
University Baptist Church	Coral Gables	FL	1,535
Victory Church	Lakeland	FL	2,000
Westside Baptist Church	Jacksonville	FL	1,197
Westside Baptist Church	Gainesville	FL	1,050
Woodland Community	Bradenton	FL	1,500

Georgia

Avalon Church   McDonough   GA   1,275

12Stone Church Lawrenceville GA 13,563

12Stone Church is an American multi-site church with multiple locations in Gwinnett County, Georgia. Kevin Myers is the founder and senior pastor of 12Stone.

As of March 2015, there are nine physical 12Stone "campuses" located in Gwinnett County, Georgia, Hall County, Georgia, and Barrow County, Georgia, along with an internet campus at live.12stone.com. 12Stone was listed in late 2010 as the #1 fastest growing church in America and as the fortieth largest church in the United States with an attendance of 9,636. 12Stone is the daughter church of Kentwood Community Church.

Average weekly attendance surpassed 10,000, making 12Stone the first Wesleyan Church to surpass this milestone.

In January 2012, 12Stone opened the Sugarloaf campus in a temporary location - Peachtree Ridge High School. In May 2012, the church broke ground on the permanent Sugarloaf location, and home of the John Maxwell Leadership Center.

Ben Hill United Methodist	Atlanta	GA	9,414
Beulah Missionary Baptist	Atlanta	GA	8,000
Blackshear Place Baptist	Flowery Branch	GA	2,635
Browns Bridge Church	Cumming	GA	6,500
Buckhead Church	Atlanta	GA	5,000
Burnt Hickory Baptist	Powder Springs	GA	2,253
Cascade Hills Baptist	Columbus	GA	4,100
Cascade United Methodist	Atlanta	GA	7,000
Central Baptist Church	Warner Robins	GA	1,050
Church of the Apostles	Atlanta	GA	3,000
Cross Pointe Church	Duluth	GA	2,001
CrossPoint City Church	Cartersville	GA	1,139
CrossPointe Church	Valdosta	GA	1,700
Crossroads Church	Newnan	GA	2,665
Dogwood Church	Peachtree City	GA	1,126
Eagle's Landing First Bapt	McDonough	GA	1,772
Elizabeth Baptist Church	Atlanta	GA	6,733

| Emmanuel Community | Conyers | GA | 1,323 |
| First Assembly of God | Griffin | GA | 7,800 |

First Baptist Church Atlanta GA 4,956

In 1848 David Gonto Daniell was sent by the Baptist State Convention to the tiny railroad town now known as Atlanta. He gathered 16 men and women together and First Baptist Church Atlanta was born. They met where they could find space, usually in a small one-room school house. In June, they dedicated their first church building on the corner of Walton and Forsyth in downtown Atlanta. Unfortunately, the building was heavily damaged during the Civil War, and many members were wounded or killed. Even still, the members trusted in God to provide a new building.

Because of Atlanta's growth, they were now surrounded by the business district and wanted to move to the suburbs north of Atlanta. They sold the Walton and Forsyth site for $81,000 and purchased a lot in the residential area across the street from the Governor's Mansion on the corner of Peachtree and Cain streets.

By 1920, once again, the church had outgrown the building and was surrounded by the business district. Sunday school had grown so much that some parents sent their children to neighbourhood churches because there was no room for them at First Baptist. When the site had been bought it was in residential area, but now the business area was closing in again, leaving no room to grow. To accommodate the current membership and provide room for growth, the church purchased an entire city block in the new residential area north of the business district at Peachtree and Fifth streets.

In 1930 the sanctuary was completed. Many people thought the building would take care of the needs of the church forever.

Dr. Charles F. Stanley was called in 1971 to be the senior pastor of First Baptist Church Atlanta. The church continued to experience tremendous growth under his teaching and leadership. By 1988, the membership had outgrown the available space again.

First Baptist Church Atlanta purchased 55 acres from the Avon Corporation in the Dunwoody area with plans to renovate the building to meet its expanded needs as a congregation.

The congregation moved to this current location, 4400 North Peachtree Road, Atlanta, GA, in April.

First Baptist Church Atlanta works continually to use the building to meet the congregation's needs. Since moving into the current location, the following renovations have been made: providing the Student Ministry with a gym and café area, expanding classroom areas in the Education wing, renovating the Children's Ministry area and building a Welcome Center for the thousands of visitors that come to First Baptist Church Atlanta each year. The Worship Center has also been renovated; the current Worship Center was completed in January 2006.

First Baptist Church	Douglasville	GA	1,000
First Baptist Church	Lilburn	GA	1,079
First Baptist Church on Square	LaGrange	GA	1,000
First Baptist Church	Powder Springs	GA	1,300
First Baptist Church	Snellville	GA	1,655
First Baptist Church	Statesboro	GA	1,071
First Baptist Church	Woodstock	GA	6,318
First Baptist	Augusta	GA	1,000
First Baptist	Bethlehem	GA	1,250
First Baptist	Conyers	GA	1,236
First Baptist	Cumming	GA	1,073

First Baptist	Gainesville	GA	1,375
First Baptist	Jonesboro	GA	2,000
First Baptist	Thomasville	GA	1,300
First Redeemer Church	Cumming	GA	1,507
First United Methodist	Marietta	GA	7,776
Free Chapel	Gainesville	GA	11,500
Glen Haven Baptist	McDonough	GA	1,154
Greenforest Community	Decatur	GA	2,000
Grove Level Baptist Church	Maysville	GA	1,500
Hebron Baptist Church	Dacula	GA	3,246
Hopewell Baptist Church	Gainesville	GA	1,005

Hopewell Missionary Baptist Norcross GA 16,000

Hopewell Missionary Baptist Church is a mega church located in Norcross, GA. Our church was founded in 1865 and is Missionary Baptist.

At Hopewell Missionary Baptist Church (HMBC), we are committed to teaching the uncompromised word of God and worshipping our Lord and Savior Jesus Christ in spirit and in truth. Hopewell Missionary Baptist Church has a dynamic, spirit-filled worship service. The Word of God is the highest priority, and it is proclaimed with power and conviction each and every Sunday morning.

The Mission of Hopewell Missionary Baptist Church is to: Fulfill the Great Commission (Matthew 28:19-20) in helping people become fully functioning followers of Christ; Teach the tenets of Christianity; Equip believers for a significant ministry by helping them discover the gifts and talents God gave them (Ephesians 4:11-16); Obey the task that has been given to us by God as a beacon of salvation living out transformational grace through His Son Jesus Christ (Matthew 5:16)

Bishop William L. Sheals, Senior Pastor, a Lakeland, FL native, came to Hopewell in May 1980. Under his direction and leadership, Hopewell grew from a small rural church to a suburban mega church. Bishop Sheals is extremely grateful to God for blessing this great union of pastor and church for 35 years, which is rarely heard of in today's religious communities.

Hopewell Missionary Baptist Church offers more than 50 ministries, including Christian education, church services, community and family outreach, pastoral, youth, and physical and spiritual wellbeing. It operates a publications and marketing department that designs, prints and markets a variety of business cards and flyers, as well as produces a weekly bulletin. The churches music and arts ministry includes choirs, dramas and dances. Hopewell Missionary

Baptist Church maintains the Hopewell Christian Academy, which works for the spiritual, mental and physical development of children. Its facilities include a sanctuary, youth center, bible institute and print shop, as well as day care and adult fitness centers. The church has a membership of more than 17,000 and also operates a bookstore. Additionally, it administers a job readiness program that includes computer training, resume preparation and interviewing skills classes

Ingleside Baptist Church	Macon	GA	1,924
Johns Creek Baptist Church	Alpharetta	GA	1,300
Johnson Ferry Baptist	Marietta	GA	4,139
Journey Church	Evans	GA	1,468
Korean Community Presbyterian	Duluth	GA	3,000
Lakewood Baptist Church	Gainesville	GA	1,500
Midway Macedonia Baptist	Villa Rica	GA	1,882
Mount Paran Church of God	Atlanta	GA	7,850
Mountain Lake Community	Cumming	GA	1,835
New Birth Missionary Baptist	Lithonia	GA	20,000
New Hope Baptist	Fayetteville	GA	1,783
North Metro First Baptist	Lawrenceville	GA	1,400

Largest Churches In The United States

North Point Community Church Alpharetta, Ga 23,377

Founded in 1995, North Point now utilizes three campuses for its weekly services. They've also planted more than 20 churches throughout the country and in Canada that serve their communities as partner churches with the flagship location in Alpharetta, a suburb of Atlanta. Andy Stanley is pastor.

Northstar Church	Kennesaw	GA	1,800
Oakwood Baptist Church	Chickamauga	GA	1,533
Peace Baptist Church	Decatur	GA	1,350
Peachtree Presbyterian	Atlanta	GA	9,000
Perimeter Church	Johns Creek	GA	4,000
Prince Avenue Baptist	Bogart	GA	1,073
Rock Bridge Community	Dalton	GA	2,880
Roswell Street Baptist	Marietta	GA	1,270

Savannah Christian	Savannah	GA	7,331
Second Baptist Church	Warner Robins	GA	1,285
Sherwood Baptist Church	Albany	GA	1,604
SouthCrest Baptist Church	Newnan	GA	2,027
Trinity Chapel Church of God	Powder Springs	GA	6,500
Victory World Church	Norcross	GA	7,500
Voices of Faith Ministries	Stone Mountain	GA	6,900
Warren Baptist Church	Augusta	GA	2,046
Watkinsville First Baptist	Watkinsville	GA	1,495
West Ridge Baptist	Dallas	GA	4,447

Word of Faith Family Cathedral Austell GA 8,300

Word of Faith began with 125 members who joined in the first service (Dec. 1991). There were approximately 350 people in the inaugural service. The ministry began with only a praise team (led by Dr. Nina Bronner), but no choir. The choir was formed by Easter of 1992. From the inception of the ministry our weekly services were broadcast on a local cable station. Our original church motto was "Each one, reach one." Sometime later, we then added the theme "Reaching the lost, teaching the found." That statement sums up the essence of the ministry. The church grew rapidly and steadily. By 2000 we were doing three Sunday morning services, each Sunday. More than forty different ministries have been added to Word of Faith since its inception. We are still endeavoring to reach the lost and teach the found! In December of 2003 Word of Faith relocated to 150 Riverside Parkway (a former Sam's Club building).

Then on Easter of 2004 Word of Faith moved across the street to 212 Riverside Parkway into its 4000+ seat Cathedral. We continue to seek to know Christ and to make Him known!

World Changers Church Int. College Park   GA   14,000

Hawaii

New Hope Christian Fellowship Honolulu HI 14,500

Wayne Cordeiro is the founding pastor of New Hope Christian Fellowship in Honolulu, Hawaii with over 14,500 in weekend attendance. New Hope is also listed as one of the top ten most innovative churches in America with Outreach Magazine listing them as one of the "top five churches to learn from." New Hope is known for redeeming the arts and technology. Over 3000 attending services each week via the Internet. New Hope has seen over 73,000 first time decisions in Hawaii since its inception 26 years ago.

New Hope Christian Fellowship, is a chartered church of the International Church of the Foursquare Gospel. New Hope International is the leadership training and church planting arm of New Hope.

Since its inception, New Hope has grown to over 124 churches in the Pacific Rim and beyond, including Las Vegas, Seattle, Simi Valley, Japan, Myanmar and Australia.

The Honolulu Star-Bulletin described New Hope as "a local personification of the nationwide phenomenon of mega-churches and the mushrooming of evangelical and Pentecostal Christianity." According to Cordeiro, "God said to me, 'Build big people, not a big church.

New Hope Leeward	Waipahu	HI	4358
Hope Chapel Kapolei	Kapolei	HI	2500
First Assembly of God	Honolulu	HI	2400
King's Cathedral Maui	Kahului	HI	5409
Word of Life Christian	Honolulu	HI	5000
Hope Chapel	Kihei	HI	2000
Calvary Chapel	Aiea	HI	1800

Iowa

Cornerstone Church	Ames	IA	2,575
Grace Church	Des Moines	IA	1,383
Valley Church	W Des Moines	IA	2000
Orchard Hill Church	Cedar Falls	IA	2000
First Assembly	Cedar Rapids	IA	2100
Prairie Lakes Church	Cedar Falls	IA	2200
Point of Grace Church	Waukee	IA	2200
Harvest Bible Chapel	Davenport	IA	2100
Faith Evangelical Free	Spirit Lake	IA	2500
Third Reformed	Pella	IA	2000

Lutheran Church of Hope Des Moines IA 10,578

Lutheran Church of Hope organized as a congregation of the Evangelical Lutheran Church in America (ELCA) in

November 1994. Since that time, Hope has become one of the fastest growing Lutheran churches in the nation, offering a wide variety of ministries for people who are searching for a new or deeper relationship with God. God has blessed Hope with a clear vision for the future, including the development of new ministries/congregations around the world and in the area.

After many months of prayer, interest meetings, and the formation of leadership teams in the fall of 2007, Lutheran Church of Hope Des Moines began worship on June 15, 2008 at Hubbell Elementary School, 800 42nd Street, Des Moines.

Hope satellites are distinctly and purposefully started and supported to reach those with no church home. Hope Des Moines is part of Hope's "one church with multiple locations," meaning it carries out the mission, vision and values of Lutheran Church of Hope – to *be a Spirited, Growing, Christ-centered Community Filled with Hope.*

Hope Des Moines is continuing to grow and reach out to a diversity of people, offering a blend of worship styles and a myriad of new ways to serve the community. This satellite is service and relationship oriented, as we continue to discover particular areas where God is calling us to serve.

On Dec. 7, 2014, Hope Des Moines moved to its permanent location at 1821 Ingersoll Avenue.

Idaho

Real Life Ministries Post Falls ID 7, 001

REAL LIFE MINISTRIES is a non-denominational Evangelical Christian church in Post Falls, situated in Kootenai County, Idaho. The church was planted in 1998 by four families, including now senior pastor, Jim Putman. Since its founding, the church has grown to an average weekend attendance of over 7,000. It has been the fastest growing non-denominational Christian church in the United States, experiencing a 247% growth from 2002-2006.

Lake City Community	Coeur D Alene ID		1925
Eagle Christian Church	Eagle	ID	2364
Capital Christian Center	Meridian	ID	3000

Calvary Chapel Boise ID 6,000

Calvary Chapel, located in Boise, Idaho, offers various community services, including education, Christmas choir and housing for homeless people. It has various ministries, including youth, nursery, interactive fellowship, school of ministry, and adult, children and outreach ministries. Its youth ministry offers Bible study for youth and senior high Bible study. Its care ministry serves various areas, such as automobile repair, budget advice, education and tutoring, furniture repair, home repair, plumbing, temporary housing for families, technical and computer support, transportation and yard work. Calvary Chapel s children s ministry organizes various events, such as summer picnic, harvest festival and Christmas events.

Vineyard Boise   Boise   ID   2200

Illinois

Apostolic Church of God	Chicago	IL	6,500
Apostolic Faith Church	Chicago	IL	4,000
Broadview Missionary	Broadview	IL	1,005
Christ Church of Oak	Brook Oak Bk	IL	5,000
Community Christian	Naperville	IL	5,400
Cornerstone Community	Marion	IL	1,079
Eastview Christian Church	Normal	IL	5500
Fellowship Miss. Baptist	Chicago	IL	8,000
Fourth Presbyterian	Chicago	IL	5,251

Harvest Bible Chapel Rolling Meadows IL 11,000

In the late 90's, God gave Harvest Rolling Meadows a vision to plant 10 churches in 10 years, so in March 2000, Pastor Ron Zappa and his wife Jody, along with 200 people, started a Harvest in Glen Ellyn. We felt God calling us to Naperville, and in October 2007, we purchased a building in Naperville and opened our doors at I-88 and Naperville Road. Since 2000, Harvest has planted over 100 churches in 14 countries.

Highpoint Ministries is the teaching ministry of Ron Zappa, providing comprehensive teaching from God's Word through weekly messages. Highpoint is also a radio teaching ministry on Chicago's Talk Radio WYLL AM 1160, Phoenix FaithTalk AM 1360, and Denver AM 990.

Pastor Ron obtained his undergraduate education in accounting and finance at Bowling Green State University and his graduate degree from Trinity Evangelical Divinity School in Deerfield, IL. He and his wife Jody live in Wheaton, IL with their three daughters Allie, Erin and Emily.

Heartland Community   Rockford   IL 7,274
Maryville First   Maryville   IL 1,420
Metro Community   Edwardsville IL 1,350

Moody Church Chicago IL 6,000

The Moody Church building is located at the corners of North Avenue, Clark Street, and LaSalle Street. It was begun in 1924 and completed 1 year later, with dedication of the building on November 8, 1925. The church melds features of both Romanesque and Byzantine architecture, and is one of the largest Romanesque churches in the US. Visually, it was intended to bridge the gap between the traditional Roman Catholic cathedral and the typical Protestant church buildings of the late 19th century and early 20th century.

The church originally was the result of the sustainable work of famed evangelist Dwight L. Moody in the mid-to-late-19th century. Moody concentrated his efforts on promoting his Sunday school, and by 1860, over 1,000 children and their parents attended each week. It had become the largest and most well-known religious outreach of its kind, with the result that President Abraham Lincoln visited the meeting one Sunday. Needing a permanent home, Moody's ministry built a 1,500-seat church at the corner of Illinois and Wells Streets, called the Illinois Street Church, which was formally dedicated December 30, 1864.

That building was completely destroyed on Sunday, October 8, 1871, when the Great Chicago Fire swept the area. The congregation immediately raised the money to rebuild, this time locating at the corner of Chicago Avenue and LaSalle Street (currently the location of Moody Bible Institute's women's dorm, Houghton Hall). The Chicago Avenue Church, which could hold up to 10,000 people, was dedicated in June, 1876. Attendance continued to climb, and on one particular Sunday, the auditorium was filled to capacity, with an additional 6,000 people standing outside the church's doors.

Dwight Moody died after an illness in 1899, and in 1908, the church was formally renamed "The Moody Church" in his honor. A.C. Dixon took over as pastor in 1906 and he stayed until 1911. In 1912, John Harper of Scotland was called to be the pastor after speaking there in a series of meetings, but tragedy overtook him before he could return to formally take up the pastorate. Returning from Scotland with his daughter and niece, Harper booked passage on the White Star Line's new ocean liner *Titanic*. Although his daughter and niece were rescued, Harper was killed in the sinking.

In 1925, the congregation moved to the Church's current location. In 1930, well-known evangelist Harry A. Ironside became the pastor, serving until his wife's death in 1948. In 1953, popular British evangelist Alan Redpath was appointed pastor, and served until 1962. From 1966 to 1971, George Sweeting served as pastor, before leaving to become the President of Moody Bible Institute, with his place being taken by Warren W. Wiersbe. On January 20, 1980, the current Senior Pastor, Erwin Lutzer, was installed as the 16th Senior Pastor of The Moody Church.

New Faith Baptist	Matteson	IL	4,400
New Life Community	E Saint Louis	IL	1,600
O'Fallon First	O'Fallon	IL	1,650
Parkview Christian	Orland	IL	7,093
Salem Baptist Church	Chicago	IL	10,100

The Compass Church	Naperville	IL	3,000
The Crossing Church	Quincy	IL	3,500
Trinity United Church of Christ	Chicago	IL	6,820
West Side Christian Church	Springfield	IL	3,500

Willow Creek Community South Barrington, Ill **25,743**

Willow Creek Community Church (or simply Willow Creek Church) is a non-denominational, multi-generational Evangelical Christian megachurch located in the Chicago suburb of South Barrington, Illinois. It was founded on October 12, 1975 by Bill Hybels, who is currently the senior pastor. The church has three weekend services averaging 26,000 attendees, making it one of the largest churches in the United States (this ranking includes multi-site churches).[1] The church has been listed as the most influential church in America the last several years in a national poll of pastors.

In addition to the South Barrington central campus, Willow Creek has 7 "regional congregations" around the Chicago area:

- Casa de Luz (Sevicio en Español in South Barrington)
- Willow Chicago (Chicago Auditorium Theatre)
- Willow Crystal Lake (Crystal Lake)
- Willow DuPage (West Chicago)
- Willow Huntley (Huntley)
- Willow North Shore (Northfield)
- Willow South Lake (Lincolnshire)

Located in a suburb of Chicago, Willow Creek was the first church to deploy giant HD screens in its theater to aid those who can't quite see the action on stage. They've also got services across an array of locations in and around Chicago.

Indiana

Christian Fellowship	Evansville	IN	2,800
Eastern Star Baptist	Indianapolis	IN	7,200
Emmanuel Miss. Baptist	Indianapolis	IN	1,000
Faith Church	Dyer	IN	4,000

Family Christian Center Munster IN 15,540

Family Christian Center is a unique, diverse, multi-cultural church with a passion to share the message of Jesus Christ to everyone and anyone - from the faceless to the famous. We are bold in our passion to share the message of Jesus in a way that speaks to our generation. Our rich history (being a part of the Northwest Indiana/Chicagoland community for over 50 years) speaks of our relentless passion to see the message of Jesus reach as many people as we can. Under the dynamic leadership of Senior Pastors Steve Munsey and Melodye Munsey, we continue to make an impact in our region and across the nation through our television broadcasts, live services and ministry resources. Our church isn't built on the gifts and talents of a few, but on the sacrifice of many. We've gained a national reputation for the innovative use of multi-media and dramatic arts. We believe the message of Jesus stays the same, but we must always be innovative in our methods of telling His story. We provide hundreds of opportunities to volunteer and serve Jesus in the area of the arts.

First Baptist Church Hammond IN 17,700

The First Baptist Church of Hammond is a fundamental Independent Baptist church in Hammond, Indiana. It is the largest church in the state of Indiana, and in 2007 was the 20th largest in the United States. Though founded in 1887 by Allen Hill, it was under Jack Hyles' leadership from 1959–2001 when it became one of the megachurches in the United States and during the 1970s had the highest Sunday school attendance of any church in the world. In 1990, the church had a weekly attendance of 20,000. It also operates Hyles-Anderson College, a non-accredited institution established for the training of pastors and missionaries, and two K-12 schools, called City Baptist Schools (for children of the bus route of the church) and Hammond Baptist Schools (for children of the members of the church). John Wilkerson is the senior pastor at First Baptist Church.

Grace Church	Noblesville	IN	6,000
Graceland Baptist	New Albany	IN	1,387
Granger Community	Granger	IN	5,500
Kingsway Christian Church	Avon	IN	2,700
Northside Christian	New Albany	IN	5,300
Second Presbyterian	Indianapolis	IN	4,000
The Chapel	Fort Wayne	IN	2,300

Kansas

Church of the Resurrection Leawood KS 15,000

The Church of the Resurrection began in 1990 with four people and a common dream. Our dream was to launch a church that would reach out to thinking people who were not actively involved in a church and help them to see how the Bible and the Christian faith could change their lives and how they in turn could change the world. From the beginning when we worshipped in the chapel of a funeral home we believed that if this new congregation was developed with excellence authenticity and relevance people would be drawn to it. Today Church of Resurrection is indeed one of America's fastest-growing churches and one of the largest churches in the Methodist community. More than 15,000 people worship study and serve here at Resurrection's campuses. Central Campus in Leawood, Kansas and Resurrection West in Western Johnson County. This year

Resurrection Downtown and Resurrection Live our Internet campus became our third and fourth campuses. From a funeral chapel to an Internet campus much has changed but our vision has never wavered. We are committed to changing lives transforming our community and renewing the mainline church. We believe that the church belongs to God and that the church is in the words of the Apostle Paul the body of Christ. The church is to be the physical presence of Christ in the world. Therefore our primary aim is to do God?s will. We believe that God has called upon the Church of the Resurrection to build a Christian community where non-religious and nominally religious people are becoming deeply committed Christians. This is accomplished through the church's vision of Changing lives transforming the community and renewing the mainline church.

Church	Location	Number
College Church of the Nazarene	O'lathe KS	3,320
Lenexa Baptist Church	Lenexa KS	2,667
Newspring Church	Wichita KS	5,481
Pathway Church	Wichita KS	3,012
Village Presbyterian Church	Prairie Village KS	4,700
Westbrook Baptist Church	Hutchinson KS	1,368

Kentucky

Bellevue Baptist	Owensboro	KY	1,326
Binghamtown	Middlesboro	KY	1,095
Florence	Florence	KY	1,194
Hawk Creek	London	KY	1,250
Highview Baptist	Louisville	KY	2,730
Hillcrest	Hopkinsville	KY	1,098
Hillview Heights Baptist	Bowling Green	KY	4,961
Immanuel Baptist Church	Lexington	KY	1,486
Little Flock	Shepherdsville	KY	1,030
Living Hope Baptist Church	Bowling Green	KY	1,940
Lone Oak First	Paducah	KY	1,341
Porter Memorial	Lexington	KY	1,013
Severns Valley	Elizabethtown	KY	1,211

Southeast Christian Church Louisville, KY 21,764

This 21,000-strong congregation in Kentucky is affiliated with the Independent Christian Churches/Churches of Christ, which differ from other autonomous Churches of Christ in the use of instrumental worship music. The church has been growing since its founding in 1962, and in 2009 opened a satellite campus in Jeffersonville, Indiana.

Southland Christian Nicholasville KY 12,524

St. Stephen Church Louisville KY 10,714

Fourteen member of Centennial Olivet Baptist Church (Louisville, Kentucky) founded St. Stephen Church in July 1926, initially met in the basement of Antioch Baptist

Church as they searched diligently for a pastor for their church. Finally, they found their pastor in the young Simmons University student, Rev. Benjamin James Miller, Sr. Rev. Miller immediately accepted the position and served as the pastor of St. Stephen Church for the next 44 years.

Rev. Miller was the first African-American to graduate from Southern Baptist Theological Seminary in Louisville, KY. He was an outstanding preacher, teacher and leader and under his anointed direction, the church grew numerically and spiritually. In 1952 a new church building was constructed on Fifteenth Street behind the existing Kentucky Street structure, to meet the congregation's growth needs. Eleven years later, the church outgrew its facility again and in January 1966 the B. J. Miller Education Building was erected on Kentucky Street. The new building was placed on the spot where the initial St. Stephen Baptist Church building stood. In November of 1979, the pulpit duties were entrusted to a 20-year-old, Eastern Kentucky University student who would eventually take the church to an even greater level of growth and ministry. The student was Kevin Wayne Cosby, grandson of Rev. Dr. B. J. Miller.

Like his grandfather Rev. Dr. Kevin Wayne Cosby was a strong proponent of education, primarily Christian education. In the mid-1980's Dr. Cosby put feet to his convictions and built a superior Sunday School Program that ignited explosive growth in the membership. By 1989, the church congregation grew beyond the initial 300 regular attendees who welcomed Rev. Cosby in 1979. Strong Sunday school classes, coupled with

Cosby's dynamic bible-based practical preaching and teaching, attracted such large crowds that hundreds of men established the "On the Wall Committee" so that women and children could be seated comfortably during Sunday morning worship service. By 1992 the congregation had grown to more than 2,000 members and the need to expand could no longer be ignored. A $1.4 million, 1,600 seat worship center was built on Fifteenth Street, adjacent to the existing worship facility. The doors were opened in September 1993. God continued to fill hearts and seats and soon the 1,600 seat worship center was too small. Attendance quickly reached 1,700 for Wednesday Night Bible Study and 7,000 every weekend, with four weekend worship services.

Valley View Church   Louisville   KY   2,150

Louisiana

Beacon Light Baptist	New Orleans	LA	8,000
Bethany World Prayer	Baton Rouge	LA	8,000
Broadmoor Baptist	Shreveport	LA	2,083
Calvary Baptist Church	Alexandria	LA	1,845
Calvary Baptist Church	Shreveport	LA	1,004
Celebration Church	New Orleans	LA	3,850
Celebration Church	Metairie	LA	4,768
Cypress Baptist Church	Benton	LA	1,011
East Bayou Baptist Church	Lafayette	LA	2,502
East Leesville Baptist	Leesville	LA	1,025

Family Worship Center Baton Rouge LA 15,540

Family Worship Center is the both the home church and physical hub of Jimmy Swaggart Ministries.

First Baptist Church	West Monroe	LA	2,246
First Baptist Church	Covington	LA	1,924
First Baptist Church	Bossier City	LA	1,750
First Baptist Church	Lafayette	LA	1,220
First Baptist Church	Houma	LA	1,016

Franklin Avenue Baptist New Orleans LA 4,760

In September of 1986 the small but faithful Franklin Avenue membership elected Fred Luter, Jr. as their pastor. This young street preacher from the Lower Ninth Ward was humbled and honored to serve this church as his first pastorate. Knowing that the congregation had been through some difficult years, this first time pastor committed himself to encourage the people by preaching, teaching, and living the Word of God! The blessings in the next few years were truly the hand and the grace of God!

* In 1988 Franklin Avenue became an autonomous church
* In 1989 a second Sunday morning service was started
* In 1993 a third Sunday morning service was added
* In March 1997 the congregation moves into their new 2,000 seat sanctuary
* In 2002 the congregation starts a satellite church in New Orleans East
* In 2003 Franklin Avenue builds a Family Life Center next to the sanctuary
* In 2005 the congregation grows to over 7,000 members
* In June 2005 the church purchases 90 acres of land in New Orleans East

On August 29, 2005 Hurricane Katrina flooded our church with nine feet of water. In January of 2006 we started having worship services in New Orleans, Baton Rouge, and Houston. Pastor Luter, while living in Birmingham traveled to these three cities as well as across the United States to minister to our displaced members.

Franklin Avenue Baptist Church was flooded with 10 feet of water during Hurricane Katrina in 2005.

In April 2008 the members of Franklin Avenue moved back into our renovated sanctuary with two worship services attended by over 4,000 members and guest! We are now one church in three cities with Pastor Sam

Young leading our Houston church and Pastor Manuel Pigee leading our Baton Rouge church.   Because of all of our displaced members our New Orleans services could be seen live over the internet every Sunday morning.

With all that we have gone through our mission remains the same which is "To Exalt the Savior", "Equip the Saints", and "Evangelize the Sinners"!

Greater St. Stephen Full Gospel New Orleans LA 10,000
Greenwell Springs Baptist Greenwell Springs LA 1,012

Healing Place	Baton Rouge	LA	8,000
Istrouma Baptist	Baton Rouge	LA	1,752
Life Center Ministries	New Orleans	LA	6,500
North Monroe Baptist	Monroe	LA	1,700
Praise Temple Baptist	Shreveport	LA	2,500
Streetlife	Baton Rouge	LA	1,100
Summer Grove Baptist	Shreveport	LA	1,109
Trinity Baptist Church	Lake Charles	LA	1,675

Massachusetts

Park Street Church Boston MA 2,000

The Park Street Church (built in 1809) in downtown Boston, Massachusetts is an active Conservative Congregational church with 2,000 in Sunday attendance and around 1,000 members [1] at the corner of Tremont Street and Park Street. The church is currently pastored by Gordon P. Hugenberger.

Park Street Church is a historic stop on the Freedom Trail. The founding of the church is predated to 1804 when the "Religious Improvement Society" began weekly meetings with lectures and prayer. The society organized the charter of the church on February 27, 1809 by twenty-six local people, mostly former members of the Old South Meeting House, who wanted to plant a church with orthodox Trinitarian theology.

The cornerstone of the church was laid on May 1 and construction was completed by the end of the year, under the guidance of Peter Banner (architect), Benajah Young (chief mason) and Solomon Willard (woodcarver). Banner took inspiration from several early pattern books, and his design is reminiscent of a London church by Christopher Wren. Park Street church's steeple rises to 217 feet and remains a landmark visible from several Boston neighborhoods. The church was the tallest building in the United States from 1810 to 1846.

The church is located adjacent to the historic Granary Burying Ground. It had its first worship service on January 10, 1810. The church became known as "Brimstone Corner", in part because of the fervent missionary character of its preaching, and in part because of the storage of gunpowder during the War of 1812.

Park Street Church has a strong tradition of missions, evangelical doctrine, and application of Scripture to social issues as well as a notable list of Firsts. Edward Dorr Griffin (1770–1837) served as the first pastor of the Park Street Church and preached a famous series of Sunday evening sermons attacking the New Divinity. In 1816 Park Street Church joined with Old South Church to form the City Mission Society, a social service society to serve Boston's urban poor.

In 1826 Edward Beecher, the brother of Harriet Beecher Stowe and son of Lyman Beecher, a notable abolitionist, became pastor of the church. On July 4, 1829, William Lloyd Garrison delivered his Address to the Colonization Society at Park Street, making his first major public statement against slavery. From 1829–1831 Lowell Mason, a notable Christian composer, served as choirmaster and organist. The church hosted the debut of My Country, 'Tis of Thee, also known as *America*, by Samuel Francis Smith on July 4, 1831. Park Street also played a role in founding the First "Homeland" or American Mission to the then Sandwich Islands (now Hawaii), where that church still stands; the Handel and Haydn Society started there. Benjamin E. Bates, an industrialist who founded Bates College in Maine in 1855, was a Sunday school teacher and active attendant of Park Street in the mid-19th century. In 1857–58 evangelist, Charles Finney led a revival at Park Street which led the pastor, Andrew Leete Stone, to experience a spiritual awakening.

Gleason Archer, a prominent inerrantist theologian was the assistant pastor of Park Street from 1945 to 1948, and his father, Suffolk University founder Gleason Archer, Sr., served as president of the Park Street Men's Club in the 1920s. In 1949 Billy Graham's first transcontinental mid-century crusade began at Park Street. Harold J. Ockenga, notable theologian and co-architect of the (Neo-) Evangelical movement was the senior pastor from 1936 to 1969, and during this time co-founded Gordon-Conwell Theological Seminary with Billy Graham, co-founded Fuller Theological Seminary, the National Association of Evangelicals, War Relief (which later became World Relief), and the Christian publication Christianity Today.

Morning Star Baptist	Mattapan	MA	2100
Calvary Chapel of Boston	Rockland	MA	3700
Church of Larger Fellowship	Boston	MA	2500
Liberty Churches	Shrewsbury	MA	2100
Grace Chapel	Lexington	MA	3000
Boston Church of Christ	Waltham	MA	2200
Jubilee Christian Church	Boston	MA	7,000

Maryland

Bethel Korean Presbyterian Ellicott City   MD 2,000
Bridgeway Community   Columbia   MD 4,000
Church of the Redeemed   Baltimore   MD 7,500
Church of the Redeemer   Gaithersburg MD 6,800
Covenant Life Church   Gaithersburg MD 6,000

Ebenezer AME Church Fort Washington MD 10,000

Since moving from the Georgetown neighborhood of Washington, DC to Fort Washington, Maryland in 1983, the church has taken many steps of faith, and God has blessed it exceedingly and abundantly. It is a tremendous story of hope. Some people call it "The Miracle on Allentown Road."

Our beginning is reminiscent of the origins of many AME churches. In 1856, 13 black members left Mt. Zion Methodist Episcopal Church in the Georgetown section of Washington, DC because of discrimination and segregation. As written by one of the founding members, they wanted to "establish a church by colored folks with colored pastors," where they would worship in dignity, spirit and truth." For a while, they erected a church at 2727 O Street NW, not far from Mt. Zion. They named it Ebenezer, meaning "stone of help," found in I Samuel 7:12. Thus began the journey of faith.

The congregation worshiped and praised God in the historic Georgetown location for well over a century. During that period, Ebenezer was blessed to have many distinguished pastors, including Rev. Charles H. Wesley, Rev. John T. Bailey, and Rev. Dr. Walter L. Hildebrand, and three pastors – Rev. Benjamin T. Tanner, Rev. James A. Handy and Rev. Alexander W. Wayman – who later became Bishops in the A.M.E Church. By 1983, black families started leaving Georgetown for economic and political reasons. Church membership fell to less than 30 people with a Sunday offering of only $200 per week. The time had come to execute the next phase of our faith walk.

With the vision, leadership and support of Bishop John Hurst Adams (the Presiding Prelate Second Episcopal District at that time), Rev. Howard C. Wright as Pastor, Dr. Joseph C. McKinney as the African Methodist Church Treasurer and the Washington Conference Board of Trustees, 17 faithful members moved to Fort

Washington, MD as the church in Georgetown was sold. Like Abraham, they moved to a land they did not know, in the midst of a people they knew not, and into an edifice that logic suggested they could not afford, but they did so in faith.

One month following the move to a 500-seat sanctuary with a $3,500 monthly mortgage note and a $300 weekly offering, our Pastors, the Rev. Dr. Grainger and Rev. Dr. Jo Ann Browning were called to serve the Ebenezer family. The congregation soon outgrew the building and began holding worship services at the Friendly High School auditorium in 1986. In 1994, having outgrown the 1,500-seat auditorium at "Friendly Ebenezer," members carried their faith pilgrimage to "Ebenezer the Beautiful," a 2,600-seat sanctuary on 33 acres of land. God indeed performed a Miracle on Allentown Road.

The Browning pastoral team has served at Ebenezer for more than 25 years. Currently, the ministry nurtures more than 8,000 members and offers 100 ministries with Bible studies, meetings and activities each day of the week. Ever mindful of the multitude of spiritual and physical needs, not just within our church family, but throughout our community, our future plans include the development of a school, family life center and senior citizen complex. Ebenezer strives to be a source of help and inspiration within the walls of the church and throughout the community.

Empowerment Temple	Baltimore	MD	10,000
Evangel Cathedral	Mitchellville	MD	4,000
First Baptist Church	Marlboro	MD	7,000
From the Heart Ministries	Temple Hills	MD	5,000
Global Mission Church	Silver Spring	MD	1,581
Immanuel's Church	Silver Spring	MD	4,000

Israel Baptist Church Baltimore MD 3,000

Since 1880, the Israel Baptist Church provides a place for Christian worship that embodies compassion and community partnering. It is a place flourishing with activity that celebrates the strength of family and the advantages of social and restorative justice in our community.

Mount Ennon Baptist Clinton MD 8,000

Reverend Delman L. Coates came to serve this church in2004 and has sought to lead the church by revitalizing the spiritual foundation of the church through relevant preaching and teaching, reverent worship, innovative ministry, and a focus on congregational care. From the very beginning of his ministry at Mt. Ennon, the church experienced considerable spiritual and numerical growth, and Pastor Coates sensed the long-term need for future expansion. In March 2004, he initiated efforts, along with Sister Barbara Palmer, to begin contacting area land owners to express the church's interest in property acquisition, and worked to prepare and position the church for the next dispensation of God's plan.

With Phase 1 of the new church complete, the church began paying its mortgage on the edifice in March 2004. To the church's dismay, however, the County had blocked construction on Phase 2 of the new church, which included the chapel, baptistery, classrooms, and offices, due to legal issues for over a year. The church's legal counsel and construction consultants had attempted to reach a resolution with the County on this matter and were doubtful a resolution could be reached. Despite their efforts, Pastor Coates, within months of his arrival at Mt. Ennon negotiated with county officials to reverse their rulings against the church and was able to obtain the required building permits to complete Phase 2 of the church's edifice Construction on Phase 2 began that summer and was completed a year later.

Pastor Coates has led the church to embrace the vision statement that we are "A Caring, Christ-centered, and Community Church, with a Kingdom Agenda." As a reflection of that vision, the church has incorporated the Mt. Ennon Development Corporation for social service and community outreach initiatives. The church has added over 4,500 new disciples, initiated support for foreign missions, expanded support for home missions, started a summer camp for youth, revitalized ministries, created new opportunities for service, implemented the Congregational Care Ministry, expanded Sunday School classes, established a Computer Training Lab, updated the church's financial management and reporting controls, doubled the church's land holding by acquiring 14 additional acres of land, and much more.

From a divinely inspired work developed in the house basement to a congregation of more than 7,000 fruitful disciples, Mt. Ennon continues to work towards the fulfillment of its purpose of growing disciples for Christ. God continues to guide and direct us as we prayerfully forge ahead ever seeking to know Him and work towards advancing the Kingdom.

New Life Wesleyan   LaPlata   MD   2,000
Oak Ridge Baptist   Salisbury   MD   1,311

Reid Temple A.M.E. Church Glenn Dale MD 7,450

Reid Temple is a growing community of faith with two campuses in Glenn Dale and Silver Spring, Maryland, and a combined membership of well over 10,000 persons. The church hosts over 80 innovative ministries designed to combat or provide comfort from the many challenging personal issues facing God's people. They include our men's, women's, singles, seniors, youth, marriage enrichment, HIV/AIDS, wellness, anger management counseling, financial empowerment, prayer, prison, street witnessing, sports, fine arts, liturgical dance, Christian education, tutorial services, and college outreach ministries.

Each Reid Temple location has its own unique features based on the diversity of its members, the kind of worship environments they strive to create, and their unique visions from God. What is identical in both locations is a shared dedication to the cause of Christ, a warm family feeling, the extension of love and grace to persons from all walks of life, and an unshakable commitment to the unadulterated Gospel of Jesus Christ. Both campuses offer a number of weekly Bible study classes and mid-week services in addition to Sunday services. An abundance of other church activities serve the spiritual, physical, educational, and emotional needs of all age groups, from children to senior citizens.

Michigan

Ada Bible Church   Ada   MI   12,000

Ada Bible Church offers programs and services providing Christian education for residents of all ages with an emphasis on the study of the Bible. The church offers worship services and has men, women, family, hospice, music, students and prayer ministries. Its budget counseling ministry provides financial counseling to individuals and couples facing financial hardships. The church has a school offering classes from grades kindergarten through five. It also has a union for college, career and community programs, home groups and praise and worship nights

Cornerstone Baptist Church	Roseville	MI	1,065
Detroit World Outreach	Redford	MI	5,500
Kensington Church	Troy	MI	15,000

Largest Churches In The United States

Mars Hill Bible Church	Grandville	MI	10,000
NorthRidge Church	Plymouth	MI	9,655
Resurrection Life Church	Grandville	MI	7,500
Triumph Church	Detroit	MI	11,600
Valley Family Church	Kalamazoo	MI	4,000
Woodside Bible Church	Troy	MI	7,174
Second Ebenezer Church	Detroit	MI	2000
Fair Haven Ministries	Hudsonville	MI	2000
First Assembly of God	Grand Rapids	MI	2400
Oak Pointe Church	Novi	MI	3000
Blythefield Hills Baptist	Rockford	MI	2020
Cornerstone United Meth.	Caledonia	MI	2000
Grace Christian	Sterling Hhts	MI	2000
Ward Evan. Presbyterian	Northville	MI	2300
Christ Memorial Reformed	Holland	MI	2800
Apostolic Church	Auburn Hills	MI	3000

Calvary Bible Church   **Kalamazoo MI   2000**

Calvary Bible Church is a wonderful, spirit-filled body of believers. Since its humble beginnings in 1929, Calvary Bible Church has been preaching the Good News of the gospel of Jesus Christ and equipping believers to live life according to the unchanging truth of the Bible, with an emphasis on evangelism and missions work both locally and abroad. Calvary is a non-denominational church; affiliated with the IFCA (Independent Fundamental Churches of America).

The tradition of strong, uncompromising, biblical preaching continues to be the hallmark of Calvary's ministries. We are committed to our mission statement of being and making disciples who display and proclaim the Lord Jesus Christ.

Central Wesleyan	Holland	MI	3000
Trinity Church	Lansing	MI	3500
Saint Lorenz Lutheran	Frankenmuth	MI	1800
Greater Grace Temple	Detroit	MI	8000
Faith Baptist Church	Waterford	MI	5600
Straight Gate Int. Church	Detroit	MI	2000
Kentwood Community	Kentwood	MI	2581
Hartford Memorial Baptist	Detroit	MI	5000
New Prospect Missionary Baptist	Detroit	MI	2000
Pioneer Memorial	Berrien Springs	MI	2500
First Wesleyan Church	Battle Creek	MI	2600
Word of Faith Int/ Center	Southfield	MI	11000
Mount Zion	Clarkston	MI	6000
Cornerstone Ev Presbyterian	Brighton	MI	1800
Brightmoor Christian	Novi	MI	2000
Faith Lutheran Church	Troy	MI	2000
Perfecting Church	Detroit	MI	4500
Mount Hope Church	Lansing	MI	4300

Calvary Church Grand RapidsMI 4500

Calvary is a Christian church in the evangelical protestant tradition, located in Grand Rapids, Michigan. Our desire is to be Christ's Church in this place: a living community of worship that is caring, serving, witnessing and maturing into the people God wants us to be.

The church is a concrete community that engages in practices such as assembling, maturing, serving, caring and witnessing. These five practices help us understand how the church's theological identity is experienced and expressed. They provide direction to both newcomers and members of Calvary as they seek to be involved in God's work here.

| New Saint Paul Tabernacle | Detroit | MI | 2300 |
| Riverview Church | Holt | MI | 2400 |

Minnesota

Bethlehem Baptist Church   Minneapolis   MN   5,000

Eagle Brook Church Hugo MN 17,091

Eagle Brook Church exists to bring people into a relationship with God through Jesus Christ, to draw them into a Christ-centered community and to help them grow in their faith. That's what drives every decision we make and guides every conversation we have.

Eagle Brook is focused on three key areas: providing teaching, music and environments that are **RELEVANT** to our people and culture; helping people experience **TRANSFORMATION**; and giving people the opportunity to take **OWNERSHIP** of their faith and their church as they grow, give and serve. Before planning a weekend service, special event or ministry activity, we ask these questions: Is it relevant? Will it change lives? Will it give people the opportunity to take ownership?

Living Word Christian	Brooklyn Pk	MN	6,680
Mount Olivet Lutheran	Minneapolis	MN	5,900
North Heights Lutheran	Roseville	MN	6,000
River Valley Church	Minnesota	MN	5,000
Wooddale Church	Eden Prairie	MN	5,000

Calvary Lutheran Church	Golden Valley	MN	2300
Calvary Baptist Church	Roseville	MN	1800
Woodland Hills Church	St. Paul	MN	5000
Crossroads Church	Woodbury	MN	2200
Emmanuel Christian	Minneapolis	MN	3500
Woodbury Lutheran	Woodbury	MN	2100
Berean Baptist Church	Burnsville	MN	2100
Evergreen Community	Bloomington	MN	2300
Cedar Valley Church	Bloomington	MN	2000
Church of the Open Door	Maple Grove	MN	3500
Prince of Peace Lutheran	Burnsville	MN	3000
Saint Andrew's Lutheran	Mahtomedi	MN	2100

River Valley Church Apple Valley MN   6,500

Pastor Rob Ketterling is the Lead Pastor of River Valley Church, which is based out of Minnesota's Twin Cities South Metro area. Starting in 1995 with just 13 people, Rob and his wife, Becca, began River Valley with a vision for church "outside the ordinary."

Today, River Valley is a thriving, growing church with over 6,500 in attendance at its 18 weekend services across nine locations with campuses in Apple Valley, Eagan, Edina Area, Faribault, Minnetrista, Shakopee, Woodbury and international campuses in Mbekelweni, Swaziland and Valencia, Spain.

North Heights Lutheran	Arden Hills	MN	2200
Shepherd Lake Lutheran	Prior Lake	MN	2000
Saint Philip Lutheran	Plymouth	MN	2000

New Hope Evangelical Free New Hope   MN 3757

New Hope Church is a large church located in the Minneapolis area in New Hope, MN. Our church is associated with the Evangelical Free Church of America A).

In April 1946, 500 leaflets were distributed throughout the community of Crystal and six weeks of persistence and prayer resulted in two children responding for Bible class at the local Village Hall. Those humble beginnings turned into what was known as Crystal Evangelical Free Church. Grateful for over 60 years of powerful ministry and looking ahead to new beginnings, CEFC officially became New Hope Church on July 1, 2007. The church continues to maintain its deep roots in biblical truth and its identity in Christ Jesus. We're a Christ centered community for all people and look forward to what God has ahead!

Grace Church	Eden Prairie	MN	5500
Substance Church	Roseville	MN	3000
Westwood Community	Excelsior	MN	3800
Shepherd Valley Lutheran	Apple Valley	MN	2200
Saint Andrew Lutheran	Eden Prairie	MN	2300

Hosanna! Lakeville MN   6600

We are Christians first and Lutherans second.

• We are members of Lutheran Congregations in Mission for Christ (LCMC) and the Alliance of Renewal Churches (ARC). We also associate with the National Association of Evangelicals, the Willow Creek Association, and Leadership Network.

• We are committed to advancing God's Kingdom everywhere, one person at a time. We freely associate with Kingdom minded partners to see the Gospel of Jesus Christ restore lives, bringing healing and freedom.

Missouri

Abundant Life Baptist	Lees Summit	MO	2,880
Crossway Baptist	Springfield	MO	1,500
Faith Church	St. Louis	MO	25,000
First Baptist Church	Raytown	MO	1,500
First Baptist Church	Branson	MO	1,208
First Baptist Church	Warrensburg	MO	1,000
First Baptist Church	Arnold	MO	2,686
First Baptist Church	Saint Charles	MO	1,288
Forest Park Baptist	Joplin	MO	1,964

James River Church Springfield   MO 12,000

James River Church (JRC) has grown from its original four families in a storefront in 1991 to a megachurch on two separate campuses. The main campus, known as James River Church - South Campus, includes multiple sanctuaries, a cafe, meeting rooms, offices, and the River Fitness Center. The second campus, James River Church - West Campus, is located off of US Hwy 60 in Southwest Springfield. A ground-breaking ceremony was held at JRC-West in fall of 2010 for further expansion at that location completed in the spring of 2013.

James River Church was founded out of the desire of the four couples to start a church on the southeast side of Springfield, a place where the Assemblies of God was not heavily represented at the time. The small congregation grew quickly and had to move into a larger space in an office park within nine months. It was at that time that John Lindell was hired to serve as pastor of the congregation. When he arrived in September 1991, he asked about expectations and the answer was "400 people in four years". However, in 1993, the average attendance topped 800. By April 15, 2008, the average attendance was 9,015, indicating a growth of approximately 1,200 people from the previous year. Attendance in 2009 grew at the same pace. By Spring 2010, weekly attendance averaged nearly 10,000.[1] Attendance at the December 7, 2014, James River Christmas set a new all-time James River Church record with 17,917 people attending services at both James River campuses. 2015 Easter services set a record attendance with over 17,000 people attending.

John Lindell remains the senior pastor at the JRC-South Campus. Curt Cook was the JRC-West Campus pastor until the spring 2011. David Lindell, John Lindell's son, is the current pastor at JRC-West Campus.

An estimated 2,200 attended the grand opening September 2009, and as of March 2010, the average Sunday morning attendance at Wilson's Creek averaged nearly 2,000.

In December of 2012 there was the Grand Opening of their new facilities. This included a 1,400 seat auditorium, kids venues, and a full youth center. These additions are funded through a campaign known as "The One Campaign", which used the slogan "One church in Two Locations." The name of this site was changed to the West campus as it is west of the HWY 65 and HWY 160 interchange as decided by the leaders.

In June 2007, James River Church launched their *Changing History Campaign*. Through this campaign, JRC-South added a 24,000-square-foot two-story addition to the children's wing and remodeled portions of the children's wing and the Realife Student Center. The estimated cost of construction was over eight-million dollars.

Saint Louis Family Church	Chesterfield	MO	6,000
Second Baptist Church	Springfield	MO	2,174
St. John Lutheran Church	St. Louis	MO	6,100
Morning Star Church	O'Fallon	MO	1945
Ridgecrest Baptist Church	Springfield	MO	1900

LifeChurch	St Louis	MO	2000
Forerunner Christian Fell.	Kansas City	MO	2000
Word of Life Church	Saint Joseph	MO	4000
Faith Church of St. Louis	Fenton	MO	4000
Central Assembly of God	Springfield	MO	2468
Vineyard Christian Fell.	Kansas City	MO	2000
Pleasant Valley Baptist	Liberty	MO	2905
Friendly Missionary Baptist	Saint Louis	MO	3500
Life Center	Saint Louis	MO	2500
Element Church	Wentzville	MO	2500
Saint John Lutheran	Ellisville	MO	2300
First Baptist Church	Arnold	MO	2385
Sheffield Family Life	Kansas City	MO	5135
College Heights Christian	Joplin	MO	1971
Twin Rivers Worship	Saint Louis	MO	2500
Colonial Presbyterian	Kansas City	MO	2200
Woodcrest Chapel	Columbia	MO	2200
Grace Church	Maryland Hts	MO	3800
Church on the Rock	Saint Peters	MO	4900
Saint Louis Family Church	Chesterfield	MO	6000
Christ Church of Oronogo	Oronogo	MO	2506
North Point Church	Springfield	MO	4500
Lees Summit Community	Lees Summit	MO	2001
Calvary Church	Saint Peters	MO	3500
Harvester Christian	Saint Charles	MO	3286
First Baptist Raytown	Raytown	MO	2000
The Crossing	Columbia	MO	3400
The Crossing	Chesterfield	MO	6000
La Croix United Methodist	Cape Girard.	MO	1943
First Baptist Church	Arnold	MO	2385
Cape First	Cape Girard.	MO	2800
The Journey Fellowship	Saint Louis	MO	3300
Abundant Life Baptist	Lee's Summit	MO	2000

Mississippi

Broadmoor Baptist	Madison	MS	2,298
Colonial Hills Baptist	Southaven	MS	1,716
Crossgates Baptist Church	Brandon	MS	1,886
Emmanuel Baptist Church	Grenada	MS	1,000
Fairview Baptist Church	Columbus	MS	1,140
First Baptist Church	Summit	MS	1,325
First Baptist Church	Jackson	MS	2,000
First Baptist Church	Madison	MS	1,050
First Baptist Church	Brandon	MS	1,059
First Baptist Church	Hattiesburg	MS	2,502

First Presbyterian Church Jackson MS   3,100

The First Presbyterian Church of Jackson has been a steadfast witness to historic, Reformed, Christianity for over 175 years.

The church's first minister was the Reverend Peter Donan (who did his studies at Princeton in the days of Charles Hodge and Samuel Miller). He and his little flock organized First Presbyterian Church on April 8, 1837, in a meeting held in the Capitol Building at the northeast corner of North President and Capitol Streets in downtown Jackson. Massive changes have occurred in our world and culture since then, but the First Presbyterian Church still holds fast "the confession of our hope without wavering.".

Dr. and Mrs. Patterson who served 1969-1983 traveled throughout the world, counseling and encouraging our growing numbers of missionaries (over 60 have come out of First Presbyterian Church). When Dr. Patterson asked to be relieved of this responsibility in 1993, his pastorate included more than 600 missionaries located in 60 countries.

The Day School is now one of the strongest programs of the church, and the church's continued growth.

Harrisburg Baptist Church	Tupelo	MS	1,107
Longview Hhts Baptist	Olive Branch	MS	1,289
Pinelake Church	Brandon	MS	9,091
Temple Baptist Church	Hattiesburg	MS	1,446
Christ United Methodist	Jackson	MS	1800
Brown Missionary Baptist	Southaven	MS	3257
The Orchard	Tupelo	MS	2300
Woodlawn Church	Columbia	MS	2500

Montana

Emmanuel Baptist Church	Billings	MT	1,065
Harvest Church	Billings	MT	2500
Faith Chapel	Billings	MT	4500

Kalispell Christian Center Kalispell   MT   2500

Kalispell's Christian Center Evolves into Canvas Church. One of the valley's oldest churches reshapes with a modern identity. Pastor Geer decided it was important to reshape the culture and identity of the church around modern times.

Two weekends ago, the 39-year-year old, now a lead pastor, formally introduced the manifestation of that goal at one of Kalispell's classic churches. The Christian Center, the prominent 75,000-square-foot site off U.S. Highway 93. The main stadium room, which seats 955 people, features a stage for a live band that plays worship songs during Sunday gatherings. Giant television screens hover overhead, helping Geer deliver his message from an informal podium where he uses an iPad for notes and presentations. A new smartphone application has been developed for the Canvas Church, which allows people to follow Bible passages, take notes and listen to Geer's past sermons. New carpet and other interior changes sweep throughout the entire campus, which includes a coffee shop, kid's nursery and an expansive auditorium for youth ministry. An additional 5,000 square feet of space is being added to the lobby in the coming months to accommodate the crowds of people who want to gather afterward.

More than 1,800 people attended the first official gathering of Canvas Church, including a large group who attended the first Spanish service that the church is now offering. As a new era begins, Geer said he is excited to see how one of Kalispell's largest, original churches makes an impact in the community. The impact, he said, will be closely tied to the church's new name, which stems from Geer's belief that, "Our lives are canvas that God displays as glory."

"God's painting in our lives and sometimes we want to be the painter and we mess it up," he said. "So when we give our life to Christ, he paints his love in our hearts and people see that. With canvas, we display God's love to our community."

North Carolina

Arran Lake Baptist Church	Fayetteville	NC	1,300
Bay Leaf Baptist Church	Raleigh	NC	1,050
Bethlehem Baptist Church	Gastonia	NC	2,287
Biltmore Baptist Church	Arden	NC	5,558
C3 Church NC	Clayton	NC	2,671
Calvary Baptist Church	Winston-Salem	NC	3,304
Calvary Church	Charlotte	NC	5,000
Center Grove	Clemmons	NC	1,043

Central Church of God Charlotte NC 8,000

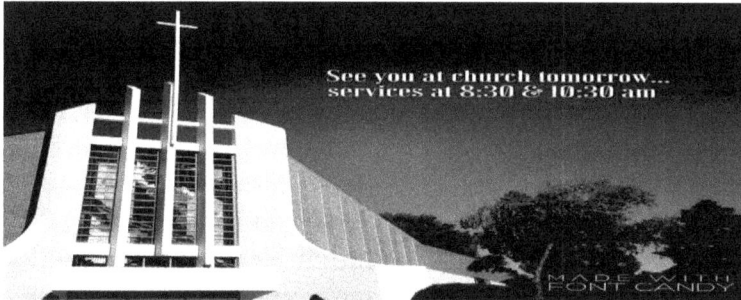

Central Church of God was chartered in January 1977. Reverend G. E. Weatherby was founding pastor, and four months later Loran Livingston became pastor. Central Church of God is a mega church located in Charlotte, NC. Our church is associated with the Church of God (Cleveland, TN) (COG). Beginning with a humble but dedicated membership of 19, no one could even imagine all that God had in store. Soon eight acres were purchased at Central

Avenue and Kilborne in Charlotte, where the first metal building was constructed. But the building didn't stop there. As the Sunday morning worship services grew to 1,600 in attendance, the facilities were expanded three times from 1977 to 1988 to accommodate the growth. Then, in 1988, the present property and facilities at Sardis Road were purchased, providing the capacity to grow to approximately 6,000 in attendance.

But the richest part of Central's compelling history has always been its people — who throughout the years have learned that real strength is found in serving and only that which is done for Christ will last.

Christ Presbyterian	Matthews	NC	2,350
Daystar Church	Greensboro	NC	1,300
Elevation Church	Matthews	NC	11,708
Englewood	Rocky Mount	NC	1,134
Faith Baptist Church	Youngsville	NC	1,200
First Baptist Church	Indian Trail	NC	2,888
First Baptist Church	Jacksonville	NC	2,608
Green Street	High Point	NC	1,039
Hendersonville First	Hendersonville	NC	1,341
Hickory Grove Baptist	Charlotte	NC	3,834
Hopewell	Monroe	NC	1,275
Lawndale Baptist Church	Greensboro	NC	1,400
Lee Park Baptist Church	Monroe	NC	1,637
Life Community Church	Jamestown	NC	1,134
Mecklenburg Community	Charlotte	NC	6,000
Mud Creek Church	Hendersonville	NC	3,220

Myers Park Presbyterian	Charlotte	NC	4,500
North Asheville Baptist	Asheville	NC	1,350
Northside	Wilmington	NC	1,100
Northside Baptist Church	Charlotte	NC	2,000
Parkwood Baptist Church	Gastonia	NC	1,313
Pleasant Garden	Pleasant Garden	NC	1,100
Scotts Hill	Wilmington	NC	1,284
Temple	New Bern	NC	1,935
The Cove Church	Mooresville	NC	5,000

The Summit Church Durham NC 6,639

The Summit began life as a church in 1961 under the name Homestead Heights Baptist Church when Sam James preached the first service at what was then the Grace Baptist Mission in Durham. Within a year, the mission had grown into the new Homestead Heights Baptist Church. The church increased to a membership of over 150 by 1965 and as it continued to grow, the congregation constructed a new church building in the 1980's to host close to 600 people. Although it briefly exceeded capacity, the 1990's saw little growth and eventually declined to a stable 400 members.

In December 2001 the church voted to call J.D. Greear as the new lead pastor. At the time, J.D. had been serving as the college pastor. Pastor J.D. immediately cast a vision for the church to engage the RDU area with the gospel. Homestead Heights was "re-launched" as The Summit Church. With a new identity, it was time for a new beginning. Worship attendance at the time was about 300, but a goal was set to have 1,000 in worship that next Easter. The members came together in a show of unified energy and focus unlike anything anyone remembered seeing before. On Easter Sunday, more than 1,100 people experienced worship at the Summit.

Within the next two years, it became clear that God had even bigger plans. By the fall of 2002, The Summit Church had college students showing up for the first time. And college students travel in packs. This was a huge answer to prayer as the church recognized that the nations were actually coming to them in the form of college students and understood that if they could reach a student, they could also reach the city, state, or country that the student would return to.

The Summit has also planted 23 churches around the United States and maintains a strong church planting residency program to equip new planters. In the coming years the church hopes to see more campuses planted around the Triangle, and more church planters sent to the nations. The best thing for a community is a healthy, gospel believing local church and the Summit is grateful to be caught up in a wave of planting those communities both here and around the world.

The church has 8 locations in the Durham area.

University Pk Bapt.	Charlotte	NC	6,000
Village Baptist	Fayetteville	NC	1,087
Western Avenue	Statesville	NC	1,082
White Mem. Presbyterian	Raleigh	NC	4,000
Word Tabernacle	Rocky Mount	NC	2,250

Nebraska

Lincoln Berean Church   Lincoln NE   6,200

Lincoln Berean is a non-denominational church in Lincoln, Nebraska with many ministries for all of its members, including adults, young adults, and kids. Within each of these ministries is a common group of members that the church also offers community for: families. The Berean Family Life ministry partners with families to help them build new skills or enhance the plan they have already made. This fall they are introducing a new Parenting Series rich with teaching and to offer a place for families to connect while raising their children.

Westside Church	Omaha	NE	1,500
King of Kings Lutheran	Omaha	NE	2400
College View Adventist	Lincoln	NE	2200

Christ Community Church Omaha NE 4200

In 1921, Dr. R.R. Brown established the Omaha Gospel Tabernacle as part of the Christian and Missionary Alliance. The first services were held just west of 20th and Douglas St.

In 1923, Dr. Brown began a radio broadcast of the first ever nondenominational religious services. By 1933, Radio Chapel Service had a weekly national audience of more than half a million. The broadcast continued for the next 53 years, becoming the longest continuous radio program on any one station in the world.

In 1976, plans were developed to move to the Old Mill Business Park on what was the western edge of the city. In 1982, Bob Thune accepted God's call to lead the congregation. During his 22 years the name was changed to Christ Community Church, the current buildings were completed, and God blessed the ministry with significant influence and growth.

Lead Pastor Mark Ashton, joined CCC in 2006 with a powerful vision to reach the city, the nation and the world with the love of Christ. In 2006 we funded and built a hospital in Mali for women and children. Since then, CCC has planted four churches in Omaha – Journey Church, New Life Church, Citylight and in 2015 New City Church. Beyond the Old Mill Campus, there are thriving ministries in North Omaha in partnership with Bridge church, in the Douglas County jail and the Online venue at cccomaha.tv was launched in 2012, broadcasting the gospel to the next generation. In 2014, our campus grew to include "The Porch" at Old Mill, which currently houses Pillar Seminary, City Care Counseling Center, and the Ministry Incubation Center for emerging ministry entrepreneurs.

| Bellevue Christian Center | Bellevue | NE | 2500 |
| Lifegate Church | Omaha | NE | 1800 |

LifeSpring Church   Bellevue NE   1,126

LifeSpring Church SBC is a Baptist church in Bellevue Nebraska. This Southern Baptist Convention church serves Sarpy County NE - Senior Pastor Steve Holdaway. - Steve is passionate about being an authentic follower of Jesus. He and his wife, Susan, grew up in the Midwest. Steve and Susan have four children: Matthew, Emily, Micah, and Elise. He has a Doctor of Ministry from Midwestern Baptist Theological Seminary, a Master of Divinity from Southwestern Baptist Theological Seminary, and a Bachelor of Arts from Baylor University. Steve served as an assoc. pastor in Arkansas and then as a pastor, church planter, and college campus pastor in St. Louis before coming to LifeSpring in 1993.

New Hampshire

Manchester Christian   Manchester   NH   2100

Bethany at Chester Road   Raymond NH 2000

Our Mission To be a Christian community where the love of God is transforming us from the Inside Out and our love for God is drawing the Outside In.

Our Vision Bethany Church is a loving community, intentionally connecting with one another, so that we may be:-Comforted by the Grace of God-Changed by the Word of God-Challenged by the Mission of God

Bethany is a member of the Evangelical Covenant Churches,

New Jersey

Bethany Baptist Church	Lindenwold	NJ	6,000
Faith Fellowship Outreach	Sayreville	NJ	10,100
Rutgers Com. Christian	Somerset	NJ	2200
Pilgrim Church	Paramus	NJ	2500
The Presbyterian Church	Toms River	NJ	2500
Jacksonville Chapel	Lincoln Park	NJ	2000
Calvary Chapel	Old Bridge	NJ	4500
Cathedral International	Perth Amboy	NJ	3000
Kingdom Church	Ewing	NJ	2500
Bethany Church	Wayne	NJ	2500
Calvary Baptist Church	Morristown	NJ	1800
Metropolitan Baptist	Newark	NJ	2500
Faith Living Christian	Pennsauken	NJ	2300
Abundant Life Family	N Brunswick	NJ	2200
Agape Family Worship	Rahway	NJ	2500
Chodae Community	Norwood	NJ	2500
Evangel Church	Scotch Plains	NJ	2117
Liquid Church	Morristown	NJ	2000
Bethany Baptist	Lindenwold	NJ	6000
Christ Church	Rockaway	NJ	5000
Gloucester Cty Community	Sewell	NJ	2500
Hawthorne Gospel Church	Hawthorne	NJ	2200
First Baptist Church	Somerset	NJ	6000
Fellowship Alliance	Medford	NJ	2500
Princeton Alliance Church	Plainsboro	NJ	1800

The church on the move

St. Matthews Baptist Williamstown NJ 13,000

Pastor Raymond Gordon, Sr. serves as Senior Pastor of St. Matthew's Baptist Church in Williamstown, New Jersey.

The doctrinal position of ST. MATTHEW'S BAPTIST CHURCH is historically that of conservative, evangelical Christianity. ST. MATTHEW'S BAPTIST CHURCH rests firmly upon the integrity and inerrancy of the Holy Scriptures and, therefore, wholeheartedly accepts the great basic doctrines of the historic Protestant Christian faith.

St. Matthew's Baptist Church (SMBC) was established in 1924 under the direction of its founding pastor, Rev. James Russell. In 1947 the church purchased the site on Glassboro Road, broke ground in 1948 and began hosting its services for its growing congregation.

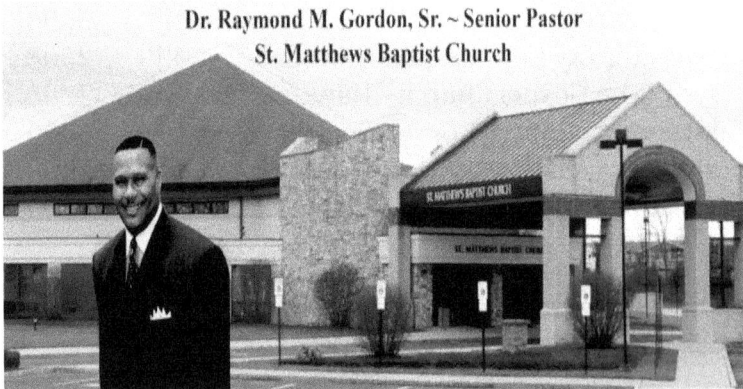

Dr. Raymond M. Gordon, Sr. ~ Senior Pastor
St. Matthews Baptist Church

New Mexico

Casa Del Rey	Albuquerque NM	3100
Legacy Church	Albuquerque NM	10,100
Mesilla Park Community	Mesilla Park NM	1,200

Sagebrush Community Albuquerque NM 10,105

One visitor said, "It is a big MEGA CHURCH I can see the size turning off people, but they have some great programs in place. You can join a small group, take some classes, or even have a conversation with someone by the entrance of the worship center.

The services are contemporary and filled with anecdotes. The senior pastor Todd is a great speaker and keeps your attention. Everyone should have a least one laugh while in church. I want to focus on the kids program. This is probable the main reason we have stayed at this church. Their kids program is top notch. My 5 year loves it. She even talks about when she can go back. They have multiple rooms and engaging activities for the kids. If I was just reviewing the kids services I would give this place 5 stars. This church allows you to build a relationship with Jesus at your own pace. There are a lot resources available.. Overall we have been happy. It took some getting used to being a MEGA CHURCH but it's been great"

CopperPointe Church	Albuquerque	NM	2000
Destiny Center Church	Rio Rancho	NM	1800
Hoffmantown Church	Albuquerque	NM	1800
Pinon Hills Community	Farmington	NM	2000
Faith Christian Family	Clovis	NM	2000
Calvary Baptist Church	Las Cruces	NM	1800

Calvary Chapel Albuquerque NM 16830

Skip Heitzig is a native of southern California and experienced the volatile days of the counterculture in the late 60s and early 70s. Though raised in a religious home, Skip saw religion as a dead-end street with no answers. As a teenager, he got caught up in drugs and ventured into the occult. But God reached Skip one day in 1973 as he was watching a Billy Graham crusade on TV. The gospel message penetrated his soul, and he knelt and prayed to receive Christ.

Skip studied under Chuck Smith at Calvary Chapel of Costa Mesa, California, until 1981. After he married Lenya, the couple moved to Albuquerque, New Mexico, where he worked in the medical field of radiology. In 1982, Skip began a home Bible study, which eventually grew into Calvary Albuquerque. In 1988 and 1989, Calvary Albuquerque was considered the fastest growing church in America. Today, Calvary Albuquerque ministers to over 15,000 people every weekend. Calvary Albuquerque has been instrumental in planting other churches, including several in Arizona, Colorado, and other parts of New Mexico.

Skip reaches out to thousands across the nation and throughout the world through his multimedia ministry, which includes a TV broadcast and nationwide half-hour radio program, *The Connection*.

We are a fellowship of believers who pursue the God who is passionately pursuing a lost world; we do this by connecting with one another, through worship, by the Word, to the world.

What We Do:
Connect Up
We express our adoration of Jesus through dynamic worship and uncompromised obedience.
Connect In
We explain the relevance of the Bible to empower and transform lives for service.
Connect Out
We extend hope to a hurting world by proclaiming the gospel and demonstrating Christ's love.
How We Do It:
Connect Up
Attend a Calvary main worship service each week.
Connect In
Actively participate in a Connect Group.
Connect Out
Actively serve in a Calvary ministry.

Nevada

Central Christian Henderson NV 21,055

Jud Wilhite serves as Senior Pastor of Central Christian Church. Under Jud's leadership, Central is dedicated to introducing people to Jesus and helping them follow Him. He is known for his conversational approach to teaching the Bible and his passion to help others know God and love Him more. Jud is a Best-Selling author who has written several books including *The God of Yes, Pursued,* and a study Bible for new believers, *The Uncensored Truth Bible for New Beginnings*. His teaching segments are heard nationally on KLOVE radio.

Here at Central, we exist to introduce people to Jesus and help them follow Him. We strive to present the basic, enduring Biblical standards and principles that people of all backgrounds can base their lives upon, and use to embrace a new life in Christ. At Central, you belong and can become all that God wants you to be.

―――――――

Green Valley Baptist	Henderson	NV	1,300
Hope Baptist Church	Las Vegas	NV	1,813
Shadow Hills Baptist	Las Vegas	NV	2,781
Summit Christian Church	Sparks	NV	2467
Living Stones Church	Reno	NV	2297
The Crossing A Christian	Las Vegas	NV	2577
Grace Church	Reno	NV	2500
Canyon Ridge Christian	Las Vegas	NV	6500
Grace Community Church	Reno	NV	2800
Church at South Las Vegas	Henderson	NV	3200
Apex Church	Las Vegas	NV	3500
International Church	Las Vegas	NV	5000
Calvary Chapel	Las Vegas	NV	3000
Victory Missionary Baptist	Las Vegas	NV	2000

―――――――

LifePoint Church Minden NV 2000

At LifePoint, we're all about loving God, Loving People and Leaving a Legacy. You matter to God, just as you are and that is why we want to welcome you to a relaxed, casual environment where you can experience God and meet other real people living real lives, just like you!

You'll experience contemporary, upbeat music and friendly people. You'll hear teaching that makes sense and is relevant to your life. You'll have opportunities to get connected with other people, when you're ready to take that step. Whether you're single, married or single again, with or without children, you will find people to connect with here at LifePoint.

At LifePoint, we believe in the importance of giving kids a fun place where they too can learn about God while they make new friends. Age-appropriate activities are provided through Rock -Solid Kids for infants through 6th grade students. Student Ministries offers junior and senior high school students with an opportunity to experience who God has designed them to be.

New York

Christian Cultural Center New York NY30,000

Dr Rev A R Bernard and his wife, Karen Bernard, teach us about the relationship we have with, Our Father! Great church 30,000 membership and growing where families are growing and extending, come, does not matter your culture is remember its "Christian Culture Center."

French Speaking Baptist	Brooklyn	NY	1,300
Greater Allen A. M. E.	New York	NY	20,000
Hillsong NYC	New York	NY	3,000
Northside Baptist Church	Liverpool	NY	1,164
Redeemer Presbyterian	New York	NY	5,000
Times Square Church	New York	NY	8,000
Full Gospel Tabernacle	Orchard Park	NY	2200
Abyssinian Baptist Church	Harlem	NY	4000
The Riverside Church	New York	NY	2500

Perfecting Faith Church	Freeport	NY	2000
The Chapel	Getzville	NY	4800
Zion Dominion Global Min.	Amherst	NY	2000
Elim Int. Fellowship	Brooklyn	NY	2000
El Centro Cristiano Adonai	Corona	NY	1900
Iglesia Macedonia	New York	NY	4550
Bethany Baptist Church	Brooklyn	NY	1800
Bridge Street AME	Brooklyn	NY	2500
Saint Paul Com. Baptist	Brooklyn	NY	2000
International Christian	Staten Island	NY	2450
Eastern Hills Wesleyan	Williamsville	NY	2500
Korean Presbyterian	Flushing	NY	3000
Grace Community Church	Washville	NY	2293
Northway Fellowship	Clifton Park	NY	2000
Concord Baptist Church	Brooklyn	NY	2500
Thessalonia Baptist	Bronx	NY	2000
Christian Faith Fellowship	Middletown	NY	2500
Christ Tabernacle	Glendale	NY	4000
The Father's House	Rochester	NY	3500
Grace Fellowship Church	Latham	NY	3400

Brooklyn Tabernacle   Brooklyn   NY   10000

The Brooklyn Tabernacle is a multicultural, non-denominational church in the heart of downtown Brooklyn. The church began with a handful of members in a small, rundown building in a difficult area of the city, and today it is a congregation of about ten thousand people who attend the weekly services. Pastor Jim Cymbala and his wife Carol, who directs the Grammy Award winning Brooklyn

Tabernacle Choir, have had the privilege to not only preach the gospel in the inner city, but also to see new churches grow out of the congregation in response to needs in other parts of the city and elsewhere in the country, as well as internationally. Because of its location, The Brooklyn

Tabernacle has a unique open door to minister to the cross-cultural melting pot of New York City. The church itself includes members from all walks of life, and diverse ethnic and national origins. Central to the growth and outreach of The Brooklyn Tabernacle has been a strong emphasis on prayer, through the Tuesday Night Prayer Meeting and the Prayer Band, which is devoted to interceding for needs from around the world.

Smithtown Gospel Tab.	Smithtown	NY	2700
Metro International Church	Brooklyn	NY	2400
Calvary Baptist Church	New York	NY	2000
Highland Church	Jamaica	NY	3000
Greater Centennial A.M.E.	Mt Vernon	NY	2100
Love Fellowship Tab.	Brooklyn	NY	2000
Abundant Life Christian r	East Syracuse	NY	2000
Upper Room Christian r	Dix Hills	NY	2200
Emmanuel Baptist Church	Brooklyn	NY	2200
Promise New York Church	Flushing	NY	3800
Bethel Gospel Tabernacle	Jamaica	NY	2000
Canaan Baptist Church	New York	NY	3000
Allen AME Church	Jamaica	NY	6150

The Wesleyan Church Hamburg NY 1900

Wesleyan Church of Hamburg is a large church located in the Buffalo area in Hamburg, NY. Our church is associated with the Wesleyan Church.

North Dakota

| Bethel Church | Fargo | ND | 2500 |

Hope Lutheran Church **Fargo ND** **5,000**

Hope Lutheran Church is a mega church located in Fargo, ND. Our church is associated with the Evangelical Lutheran Church in America (ELCA).

Hope Lutheran is one congregation serving two locations unified in mission. This unity multiplies Hope Lutheran's efforts to reach out to our community and our world with the good news of Jesus Christ.

Stephanie Tollefson, 35, a pastor at Hope Lutheran Church, which welcomes some 5,000 worshippers weekly. "People say a generous heart is a happy heart, and I see that here. The more you connect with other people, the more joy you get back," she says. "And the more joy you have, the more you want to give back." In Fargo, she says, "people genuinely seem to want to belong to something that's bigger than just themselves."

Ohio

514 Church	New Albany	OH	1,225
Apex Community Church	Kettering	OH	2,300
CedarCreek.tv	Perrysburg	OH	9,155
Cornerstone Church	Toledo	OH	4,000

Crossroads Church Cincinnati   OH   16,792

Crossroads is one church in five locations. In 1995, a group of 11 Cincinnatians felt a need. They wanted a great environment to meet with friends to explore questions about God without having to pretend they had it all together or wading through a bunch of religious lingo. They wanted to offer their friends an alternative that wouldn't make assumptions about what they believed about God or knew about the Bible. They wanted to assure their friends that no one would single them out by asking, "Where are all the visitors?"

On March 24, 1996, Crossroads Community Church "went

public" in a rented room at Peoples Middle School (now Clark Montessori) in Hyde Park. About 450 people showed up that day, intrigued by the promise of "great music, free coffee and real topics." In the years since, Crossroads has grown tremendously. The goal was never size; the goal always was, and continues to be, based upon the ideas of authentic community, honest conversation and exploring the question: Where is God taking us next?

So where is Crossroads going? Only God really knows. But our short history has shown us that it's a journey of creating something that hasn't yet been seen, saying things that aren't being said and trusting God to do something truly meaningful in and through a bunch of imperfect people. We've seen that kind of faith and dependence affect people within our community, our city and, increasingly, our world. We expect God to continue to lead us through hard decisions that challenge the status quo. We'll do these things because we believe that God uses them to bring all of us into a thriving life of freedom. And we're all about that.

Cuyahoga Valley	Broadview	OH	1,986
Genoa Baptist Church	Westerville	OH	1,429
Ginghamsburg Church	Tipp City	OH	5,000
Jersey Baptist Church	Pataskala	OH	1,552
LifePoint Church	Lewis Center	OH	1,275
Spring Hills Baptist	Granville	OH	1,030
First Baptist Church	Vandalia	OH	1,150
Vineyard	Cincinnati	OH	7,000

Vineyard Westerville OH 7,827

Church planting is at the heart of Jesus' call to "Go and make disciples of all nations."

Over the past 26 years, Vineyard Columbus has given away its best leaders and resources in order, as our mission statement suggests, "to develop a community of disciples who experience God, love one another, and partner with Christ to heal the world." We are a church that plants other churches to further this mission.

Throughout our history, we have planted over two dozen churches, both domestically and internationally, and we're not stopping there. In 2013, we launched the "20 in 10 Initiative" through which Vineyard Columbus has committed itself to plant 20 churches over the next 10 years. We are looking for women and men who have a passion and a call to plant Vineyard churches. If you're interested in being a lead pastor of a church plant or part of a church planting team, we'd encourage you to take your first steps toward planting and look at Our Process.

If you're considering church planting, Vineyard Columbus offers a variety of opportunities for hands-on training. We would specifically highlight our Church Planting Residency Program as a great opportunity to learn from Vineyard Columbus leaders and others in the Vineyard Movement.

This church offers way and means in teaching and training those who attend. They offer things an average church does not have, such as: Church Planting, Community Center, a way to Connect, a Counseling Center, Empowered Life, a Financial Ministry, and Fusion High School, Fusion Middle School. Classes on International Ministries, Marriage & Family Life. Men's Life. Women's Life, Singles. Small Group Community Life. Support for Life.

And has Urban Ministry, Value Life, Vineyard Institute, VineyardKids, Volunteer Ministry, bookstore and a Global Café

The main campus is in Westerville but has locations in a variety of locations in the Columbus area.

World Harvest Church Columbus OH 13,000

World Harvest Church Columbus began as a backyard Bible study in 1977. Seventeen people attended. Nobody there thought it was going to be a *church*.

But after a few meetings, the idea of something more permanent took hold. The group rented facilities in the area for weekly meetings, and eventually constructed a building on Wright Road just outside Pickerington, Ohio. The church kept growing, and eventually required a larger building on the same property. Finally, the church – then known as Word of Life – purchased property on Gender Road in southeast Franklin County, and built what is now WHC Columbus on what had been a corn field. When the new building was dedicated, the congregation was named World Harvest Church in honor of Dr. Lester Sumrall, who had befriended Pastor Rod Parsley some years earlier and had become the young pastor's mentor.

The Columbus campus of World Harvest Church also houses Harvest Preparatory School, a K-12 educational institution, the operational offices of Breakthrough, Pastor Rod Parsley's worldwide television program & six other national ministries. The Columbus campus is also the home of Valor Christian College's classrooms and dormitories.

Today, more than 12,000 people in central Ohio will tell you World Harvest is their church home. At every WHC service you'll find a family-friendly congregation of Spirit-filled believers in Jesus Christ, representing every age, ethnic group and walk of life.

Parsley was born in Cleveland, Ohio, and was raised primarily in the Columbus area. His parents grew up in eastern Kentucky, and traveled there often to visit relatives when Parsley was a young boy. Young Parsley was raised as a Free Will Baptist, and had a "born-again" experience at Christian Center Church in Gahanna, Ohio, in the 1970s. After high school, he worked in real estate and at a pet-food factory before enrolling at Circleville Bible College (now Ohio Christian University).

Grace Church	Middlebg Hts	OH	3600
Cleveland Baptist Church	Cleveland	OH	2010
Christ's Church At Mason	Mason	OH	2519
Apex Community Church	Kettering	OH	2500
NewPointe Community	Dover	OH	3200
Akron Baptist Temple	Akron	OH	3000

Largest Churches In The United States

RiverTree Christian	Massillon	OH	2600
Faith Family Church	Canton	OH	3000
First Church of God	Columbus	OH	4000
Canton Baptist Temple	Canton	OH	1800
CedarCreek.tv	Perrysburg	OH	9155
Church of the Open Door	Elyria	OH	2500
Christ Emmanuel Christian	Cincinnati	OH	2000
Far Hills Community	Dayton	OH	2000
Montgomery Community	Cincinnati	OH	2500
Fairfield Christian Church	Lancaster	OH	2000
Cuyahoga Valley Com.Ch.	Broadview	OH	2000
Lima Community Church	Lima	OH	1888
New Life Church	Gahanna	OH	1800
Cornerstone Church	Toledo	OH	4000
Shiloh Baptist Church	Dayton	OH	2500
Grace Church	Norton	OH	4000
Only Believe Ministries	Botkins	OH	2000
United Methodist Church	Reynoldsburg	OH	2200
Solid Rock Church	Monroe	OH	4000
Heritage Christian Church	Westerville	OH	2700
The Word Church	Cleveland	OH	7000
Lincoln Heights Baptist	Cincinnati	OH	3200
Upper Arlington Lutheran	Columbus	OH	2200
Crossroads Community	Mansfield	OH	5500
Columbus Christian Center	Columbus	OH	2500
Xenos Christian Fellowship	Columbus	OH	5000

The Chapel   Akron   OH   7347

Rev. Knute Larson, said the time to leave his post as co-senior pastor of The Chapel will leave after more than 25 years of leadership that has motivated the spiritual and physical growth that has made the 8,000-member church the largest in Summit County, with campuses in Akron, Kent and Green.

The nondenominational church offers six worship services and more than 300 weekly activities. Although the membership meets in three locations, the church has one staff, one budget and one mission.

"This was a strong church when I came, and it is a strong church now — teaching and seeking to practice Scripture with gracious balance. God has been very good to us," Knute Larson said. "I had one main goal when I came and it is the same right now and will be for all my life: to clarify for people what the grace of God means so that they can make an intelligent decision and response about Christ and to try to teach and model how that grace shows in daily life and love."

Larson, who turned 68 announced his retirement during a members' meeting in the worship center at the Akron campus. The meeting was live-streamed to those in attendance at the Green worship center. After the meeting, an e-mail blast was sent to the membership and a letter written by Larson was posted on the church Web site,

Members of the congregation have been anticipating Larson's retirement, when the church chose the Rev. Paul Sartarelli, the founding pastor of Kent's Riverwood Community Chapel, to succeed him as senior pastor. Sartarelli began as associate senior pastor and became co-senior pastor with Larson in 2007.

Larson said his decision to retire is based on his heartfelt belief that The Chapel family is ready for its next leader, and that Sartarelli is that person.

Sartarelli credits Larson for a smooth transition.
"Pastor Larson really did a good job of preparing the people for this announcement, and they are ready to continue our ministry," Sartarelli said. "I'm grateful for what he started and what he has done, and I am excited to see what the future holds for The Chapel. I am humbled to be the leader going into that future."

Before planting the Kent church, a daughter church of The Chapel, Sartarelli spent eight years on staff at The Chapel as an intern.

Christian Life Center	Dayton	OH	2700
Grace Brethren Church	Westerville	OH	2500
Christ Community Chapel	Hudson	OH	4500
SouthBrook Christian	Miamisburg	OH	3100
New Salem Baptist Church	Columbus	OH	2000

Cypress Wesleyan Church Galloway OH 3200

Cypress Wesleyan Church is a mega church located in the Columbus area in Galloway, OH. Our church is associated with the Wesleyan Church.

Cypress Wesleyan Church offers 5 weekend worship services, including services on Saturday evening and additional services at one of our alternative locations.

Originally located on Cypress Ave. in downtown Columbus, Cypress has a great family history of reaching people far from God, helping people grow in their faith, and serving others as a way of serving God.

We exist to connect people closer to Christ and one another by REACHING those far from God, GROWING people in their journey with Christ, and SERVING others in the name of Christ.

Man's Authentic Nature	Loveland	OH	4000
The House of the Lord	Akron	OH	3000
Victory Christian Center	Lowellville	OH	2500
Fairhaven Church	Centerville	OH	3500
First Christian Church	Springfield	OH	2074

Grove City Church of Nazarene Grove City OH 3446

The NAZ is the place for the community of Grove City to connect with each other and with the resources that grow healthy people and strong families. Whether your need is spiritual, physical, emotional, or relational, The Naz is the place to help you take your next steps...

The Saturday evening worship experience is set in an intimate and casual atmosphere allowing you an opportunity to experience reverent worship and celebrate the goodness of our Lord. During this time you will be led by an amazing team of worshipers who give of their time and lives to see God glorified.

Sunday 9am - Classic Experience

The Sunday 9am worship experience is a culture of warm and friendly people committed to making our worship exciting and life-changing. Every generation gathers together before our Great Creator in worship.

We desire to clearly sense and experience God's presence every time the church gathers. We want to connect intimately with Him and hear His voice so that more of His character and nature can be found in us! This service features classic worship, a modern-day gospel sound, and fresh presentations of standard worship hymns led by the GCCN choir and band.

Worship is one of our core foundations. Our desire is to use music to help people connect with God in a greater way. We are committed to expressing our love to our Lord and Savior who is worthy of all praise.

Sunday 11am - Contemporary Experience

The Sunday 11am worship experience is a community of worshipers seeking an authentic encounter with God. Our service presentation offers an artistic atmosphere conducive to both praise and worship. Through alternative musical textures, sincere lyricism, and creative presentation, God is able to connect directly to his people, wherever they may be.

Mount Zion Baptist   Oakwood Vill OH   3000

Parkside Church Chagrin Falls OH 4000

We are a community of believers in the east suburbs of Cleveland. We strive to bring God glory through singing, hearing His Word preached, loving Him and loving one another.

We're glad that you're here. We invite you to spend some time getting to know us, and we hope that you'll come away from this site encouraged to join us at Parkside this week.

This church as additional locations.

Olivet Institutional Baptist Cleveland   OH   2000
Vineyard Christian Fell.   Beavercreek OH   3000

The Chapel   Sandusky OH 2200

We know it can be a little overwhelming when you walk through the door for the first time in a new place. We've been there, and that's why we want to make sure the opportunity for you to take a step forward is always at your own pace.

Our **Second Glance Lunch** is a great first step to take, with its relaxed atmosphere and the chance to meet some of The Chapel pastors and staff. If you're looking for a more in-depth look at our church, check out our 8-week **Foundations: Beginning** class taught by lead pastor, Bill Schroeder.

The Chapel offers a huge variety of **Connection Groups** - from motorcycling to golfing and bible studies to couples or singles groups - you can find a Connection Group that fits your interests and passions. Connection Groups may meet here at the church or in other locations in the surrounding area, and vary in size.

Some groups equip us to grow, while others draw on common interests or offer support. There are **Connection Groups** for women, men, young adults and singles.

Oklahoma

LifeChurch.tv Edmond, Ok 26,776

In January 1996, Life.Church began in Oklahoma City with 40 congregants meeting together "in a two-car garage, equipped with just a borrowed overhead projector and two construction lights purchased at Lowe's for $19.99." From 1996 to 1999 the church membership grew rapidly. During this time, Life.Church acquired its first facility (now known as the "Oklahoma City Campus"). In 2001, MetroChurch, a 25-year-old, nondenominational church in nearby Edmond, Oklahoma joined with Life.Church, effectively making it a multi-site church. Following the success of the additional location, the church launched campuses in Tulsa, Oklahoma and Stillwater, Oklahoma in 2002, and these new campuses began incorporating satellite video teaching into their services.[5]

Life.Church opened an additional campus in OKC, the South Oklahoma City Campus, in Spring 2005. In February 2006, Life.Church introduced a campus in Fort Worth, Texas. In April, the church established its "Internet Campus," which broadcasts weekly, interactive worship services live over the internet. In July, the church also launched a new campus in Hendersonville, Tennessee.

Easter Sunday, 2007, Life.Church began broadcasting from their new campus in the online game Second Life.

Life.Church also decided to do away with "church membership", deciding instead to encourage people to become "partners" in helping lead people to become fully devoted followers of Christ. The church has developed a Bible application for mobile phones, YouVersion. Introduced in 2008, it has been described as "[t]he world's most popular Bible program for mobile phones."

Life.Church features a casual dress code and most attendees wear jeans and casual clothing, the worship service includes refreshments before and after the services, music style is pop-rock and praise-worship, with the performances amplified concert style and lyrics shown on projector.

First Church Nazarene	Bethany	OK	4,789
Bethel Baptist Church	Norman	OK	2,369
Church of the Servant	Okla City	OK	7,495
Church on the Move	Tulsa	OK	11,000
Emmanuel Baptist Church	Enid	OK	1,370
First Baptist Church	Moore	OK	1,400

First Baptist Church	Tulsa	OK	1,451
First Missionary Baptist	Ardmore	OK	1,179
Immanuel Baptist Church	Shawnee	OK	1,800
Journey Church	Norman	OK	5,000
Newchurch	Okla City	OK	1,000
Quail Springs Baptist	Okla City	OK	1,730
South Tulsa Baptist Church	Tulsa	OK	1,035
Southern Hills Baptist	Okla City	OK	1,445
Rhema Bible Church	Tulsa	OK	5500
Victory Church	Okla City	OK	8000
First Baptist Church	Okla City	OK	2000
Southwest Baptist Church	Okla City	OK	2500
First Baptist Church	Edmond	OK	2000
Crossroads Cathedral	Okla City	OK	2500
Mem. Rd Church of Christ	Edmond	OK	2600
Victory Life Family Center	Durant	OK	4000
Boston Ave. U Methodist	Tulsa	OK	2004
Asbury United Methodist	Tulsa	OK	3274
Westmoore Community	Okla City	OK	2000
People's Church	Okla City	OK	6000
Faith Tabernacle	Okla City	OK	2000

Victory Christian Center   Tulsa OK   9500

Paul Daugherty, along with his wife Ashley, serve as the Lead Pastors of Victory in Tulsa, Oklahoma. Paul speaks weekly at Victory's services ministering to audiences through TV and podcast; reaching thousands of people with God's Word. He and Ashley also travel around the world speaking at churches, conferences and crusades. His style of preaching is described as refreshingly transparent, encouraging, and practical. Paul's desire is that people feel empowered and challenged to step out and fulfill God's purpose for their lives.

Paul is the author of the mini book titled, "The Fourth Quarter" which encourages you to finish strong no matter what season of life you are in. He has written worship songs that are featured on several albums, and has also released two personal albums, which have appeared on TBN and Daystar global television on the 360 Life television series. Paul is a graduate of Oral Roberts University, with a bachelor's degree in Theology, and is currently working on his Master's Degree at Oral Roberts University.

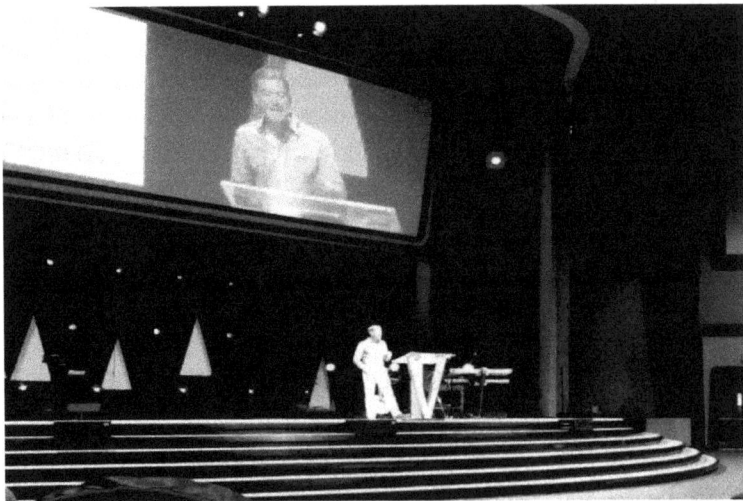

Cathedral of Praise	Okla City	OK	1800
First Baptist Church	Broken Arrow	OK	2100
Church at Battle Creek	Broken Arrow	OK	2092
Crossings Community	Okla City	OK	5500

Largest Churches In The United States

Guts Church	Tulsa	OK	4000
Destiny Church	Broken Arrow	OK	1800
Church of the Harvest	Okla City	OK	2500
Church of the Servant	Okla City	OK	1992
Council Road Baptist	Bethany	OK	2300
Henderson Hills Baptist	Edmond	OK	2500
Grace Church	Broken Arrow	OK	1800
First Baptist Church Altus	Altus	OK	2000
Broken Arrow Baptist	Tulsa	OK	2092

Oregon

Beaverton Foursquare   Beaverton   OR 6,000
City Bible Church   Portland   OR 7,000
Southlake Foursquare   West Linn   OR 3,500

Grand View Baptist Beavercreek OR 1,100

Grand View is an independent Baptist church pastored by Dr. Mike Mutchler who founded the church 29 years ago. It has a friendly, family atmosphere, compassionate vision, and strong commitment to Bible truth. The church has three locations and a Spanish congregation. Pastor Mutchler started the Church at 29 and is now 61. His plan, Lord willing, is to pastor the Church until he is 70 years old and then be on staff helping the site Churches flourish. We have an excellent staff with 10 pastoral staff including two site pastors and our Spanish Pastor. We have about 40 employees in Church and Grand View Christian Academy combined. Our income for 2015 will go over 2,000,000 for the year.

The Church had a high weekend last year of six services on property with 3,860 people and 970 being saved. The single largest day on Sunday in Sunday school was 1,856 with 540 trusting Christ. Not counting any large days, which we have a few times a year, we would average 1,150 for Church and a hundred or so less for Sunday school. We are in Beavercreek, Oregon which is not even a city, but a Hamlet.

Dr. Mutchler is author of *"Building Your Church From the Ground Up"*.

Cedar Mill Bible Church	Portland	OR	1900
Solid Rock Church	Portland	OR	6000
Morning Star Community	Salem	OR	2500
Portland Christian Center	Portland	OR	2000
Salem Alliance Church	Salem	OR	2600

Rolling Hills Community Tualatin OR 2900

We are a group of diverse people united in our commitment to...

Reach the world one person at a time, as we learn to think, love, and live like Jesus, and to reproduce that in the lives of others.

We seek to be in real community together, where it's safe to be known and walk alongside each other as we pursue Jesus. When we are in genuine relationships with others who are being guided by Jesus, as revealed in the Bible, God transforms us. He takes what is broken in us and makes it whole. As we experience our own love relationship with God, our heart for the needs of others cannot remain indifferent. As a church family, we are motivated to move toward the people and needs in our community with love and compassion.

We believe God is at work in us, as well as through us, to positively impact our community, region, and world.

First Church of Nazarene	Salem	OR	2000
Good Shepherd Community	Boring	OR	2300
Westside Church	Bend	OR	3500
Sunset Presbyterian	Portland	OR	2300
Abundant Life Church	Damascus	OR	2426
First Baptist Church	Eugene	OR	3000
Applegate Christian	Jacksonville	OR	7000
Imago Dei Community	Portland	OR	2000
Table Rock Fellowship	Central Point	OR	2000
East Hill Foursquare	Gresham	OR	2800

Pennsylvania

Bryn Mawr Presbyterian	Bryn Mawr	PA	2,800
Calvary Chapel	Philadelphia	PA	14,000
Covenant Fellowship	Glen Mills	PA	4,000
Deliverance Evangelistic	Philadelphia	PA	11,000
Enon Tabernacle Baptist	Philadelphia	PA	15,000
First Presbyterian Church	Bethlehem	PA	2,600
Korean United Church	Philadelphia	PA	1,500
LCBC	Manheim	PA	13,854
Sharon Baptist Church	Philadelphia	PA	4,494
Tenth Presbyterian	Philadelphia	PA	2,361

Yuong Sang Presbyterian Horsham PA   5,000

Eternal Life Ministries ("ELM") is a ministry of Yuong Sang Presbyterian church located in the greater Philadelphia area. We invite you to come worship with us at our Sunday service and visit the welcoming table before service as we look forward to meeting you personally.

Pocono Community	Mt Pocono	PA	2000
King Street Church	Chambersburg	PA	2000
The Bible Chapel	McMurray	PA	2500
Christian Life	Camp Hill	PA	2900
Bright Hope Baptist	Philadelphia	PA	2000
Dove Christian Fell.	Ephrata	PA	2000
North Way Christian	Wexford	PA	3000
Calvary Church	Lancaster	PA	2500
The Worship Center	Lancaster	PA	2150
Mount Ararat Baptist	Pittsburgh	PA	4800
Lives Changed By Christ	Manheim	PA	13854
Greater White Rock Baptist	Philadelphia	PA	3000
Christian Life Center	Bensalem	PA	1900
Covenant Church	Pittsburgh	PA	2000
Victory Family Church	Cranberry	PA	2000
Glad Tidings Church	Reading	PA	2689
Church of the Saviour	Wayne	PA	2000
Parker Hill Community	Scranton	PA	1950
Allegheny Center Alliance	Pittsburgh	PA	2700
Calvary Fellowship	Downingtn	PA	2000
Living Word Community	York	PA	2500
West Shore Evangelical Free	Mechanicsbg	PA	2500
Christian Stronghold Baptist	Philadelphia	PA	2500
Calvary Church	Souderton	PA	2100
Pocono Community	Tobyhanna	PA	1855
Worship Center	Lancaster	PA	2500
Greater Shiloh Church	Easton	PA	2300
Lifechurch	Allentown	PA	2000
Sharon Baptist Church	Philadelphia	PA	5000
Evangelical Free Church	Hummelstn	PA	2000

South Carolina

Alice Drive Baptist	Sumter	SC	1,338
Anderson Mill Road Baptist	Moore	SC	1,291
Bible Way Church	Columbia	SC	7,000
First Baptist Church Boiling	Springs	SC	1,508
Brookland Baptist Church	West Columbia SC		8,075
Brushy Creek Baptist	Taylors	SC	1,161

Cedar Creek Baptist Church Aiken SC   7,734

Our mission is to help people find their way back to God. We try to accomplish this task by doing two things really well: our Sunday services and our small groups. Each Sunday, thousands of people attend one of our contemporary, creative and biblically-driven worship services for adults, students, children and pre-school age kids. We hope to connect people in small groups where they can experience real relationships with real people for real life change.

Historically, we are one of the oldest churches in this region. Established in 1792, our history goes back to the earliest days of the United States when pioneers like Daniel Boone crossed the Appalachian Mountains in search of new land. Only 16 years younger than our nation, our church was established the same year that Kentucky became a state. Very few churches enjoy such a long and storied history as ours. While we look backwards with great fondness, we believe our wonderful heritage lays a foundation for an even more prosperous future!

Denominationally, we are a Southern Baptist church. That means that we are in friendly cooperation with other Southern Baptist churches. The principle areas in which this cooperation is demonstrated is in our united efforts for missions and theological education. While we do cooperate with non-SBC churches, the level of cooperation depends upon the level of our agreement on important theological and cultural issues. In other words, our level of participation will correspond to our level of agreement.

This church has three campuses in the area.

Clearview Baptist Church	Travelers Rest	SC	1,000
First Baptist Church	Columbia	SC	2,100
Cornerstone Community	Orangeburg	SC	1,250
Foothills Community	Seneca	SC	1,500
Fort Mill First Baptist	Fort Mill	SC	1,100
Grace Church	Greenville	SC	5,000
Millbrook Baptist Church	Aiken	SC	1,036

NewSpring Church Anderson SC 31,805

NewSpring is a church where change takes place. Rather than being a building where people far from God are met with shame, guilt, and condemnation, Jesus leads us to be a family that extends His grace, mercy, and forgiveness to everyone. No matter what you've been through or what questions you might have, we want you to be a part of the family.

The NewSpring Network is an online community designed to equip churches reaching people far from God. We help develop and resource leaders with tools for Jesus-centered leadership and living.

NewSpring College Leaders in the church today face the challenge of engaging a culture that has written off religion and the local church. We still believe Jesus is the hope of the world, and we want to raise up a generation of leaders to take the gospel to the world through the local church.

It is the second fastest-growing and fourth largest church in the Southern Baptist Convention. Overall, it is among the one hundred fastest-growing and largest churches in the United States and it is ranked as the second fastest-growing church in the United States.

In addition to the church in Anderson, NewSpring's other locations in South Carolina include, Aiken, Boiling Springs, Charleston, Clemson, Columbia, Florence, Greenville, Greenwood, Myrtle Beach, Powdersville and Spartanburg. The goal of this church is to reach 100,000 people to become active in their church. Perry Noble is the head pastor.

North Augusta First Baptist	N Augusta	SC	1,013
North Spartanburg First	Spartanburg	SC	2,000
Old Fort Baptist	Summerville	SC	1,101
Rock Hill First Baptist	Rock Hill	SC	1,000
Rock Springs Baptist	Easley	SC	2,500
Seacoast Church	Mt Pleasant	SC	9,200
Shandon Baptist Church	Columbia	SC	2,250
Simpsonville First	Simpsonville	SC	1,984
Spartanburg First Baptist	Spartanburg	SC	3,400
True North Church	N Augusta	SC	1,650
Lexington Baptist Church	Lexington	SC	1800
Brookwood Church	Simpsonville	SC	6103

Freedom Temple Min.   Rockhill   SC   2200

Redemption World O. C.   Greenville   SC   10550

Redemption World Outreach Center is a mega church located in Greenville, SC. Our church was founded in 1991 and is Non-Denominational / Independent.

Leaders: Apostle Ron Carpenter, Co-Founder and Senior Pastor. Apostle Hope Carpenter, Co-Founder and Senior Pastor

Largest Churches In The United States

Word of God Church	Columbia	SC	2200
Faith Assembly of God	Summerville	SC	2305
First Baptist Church	Simpsonville	SC	2081
First Baptist Church	Taylors	SC	2300
Marathon Church	Greenville	SC	2500
Church of the Holy Cross	Sullivan's Isd	SC	1800
Riverbend Baptist Church	N Charleston	SC	3500
First Baptist Church	Columbia	SC	3500
Transformation Church	Indian Land	SC	2500
Grace Church	Greenville	SC	4000
First Baptist North	Spartanburg	SC	2600
First Baptist Church	Spartanburg	SC	3200
Barefoot Church	N Myrtle B	SC	2000
Bible Way Church	Columbia	SC	7000
West End Baptist Church	Rock Hill	SC	2000
East Cooper Baptist	Mt Pleasant	SC	2166
Shandon Baptist Church	Columbia	SC	2500
Southside Fellowship	Greenville	SC	2000
Cedar Creek	Aiken	SC	3000
Northside Baptist Church	W Columbia	SC	2000
Grace Cathedral Ministries	Greenville	SC	2000
Cornerstone Community	Orangeburg	SC	2000
Rock Springs Baptist	Easley	SC	2500
Cathedral of Praise	Charleston	SC	2700
Praise Cathedral C of God	Greer	SC	2000
Morningstar Fellowship	Fort Mill	SC	2500
Community Bible Church	Beaufort	SC	2000

South Dakota

Celebrate Church   Sioux Falls   SD   3500

In the summer of 1999 we surveyed the evangelical churches of Sioux Falls (a total of 100 churches, including all mainline denominations) and discovered approximately 32,000 people attend church on any given Sunday, with an average age of 45. (For the record, at the time of the study Sioux Falls was approximately 125,000 people with an average age of 32.8). Thus, on any given Sunday in the greater Sioux Falls area over 92,000 people are not in church, and of the 100 churches only 7 reported that their average age was under 35 (of which Celebrate is one).

In the September issue of the Argus Leader (2003) it was reported that Lincoln County is the 3rd fastest growing county in the country. The same issue reported that our city planners are expecting 65,000 new residents by 2025. There is a lot of work to be done and we wholeheartedly believe that God has called Celebrate to reach the thousands, to teach them, equip them, and ultimately release them for the glory of God.

We believe that God has called us to share in the harvest alongside the other evangelical churches that stand upon the Word of God. It is not our desire to duplicate what other churches are already doing, but to discover, and live out, our God-designed uniqueness.

Tennessee

Abba's House	Hixson	TN	2,000
Bayside Baptist Church	Harrison	TN	1,300
Belle Aire Baptist Church	Murfreesboro	TN	1,010

Bellevue Baptist Church   Memphis   TN   6,806

Bellevue Baptist Church is a large Southern Baptist megachurch in the Cordova area of Memphis, Tennessee, United States. Bellevue is the largest church in Memphis and is one of the leading churches in the Southern Baptist Convention. Bellevue's goals are to "Love God, Love People, Share Jesus, and Make Disciples." The church's head pastor has been Dr. Steve Gaines since 2005.

Bellevue Baptist was founded in 1903 by Central Baptist

Church as a mission church on the outskirts of Memphis. With a small $1,000 gift from member Fannie Jobe, pastor Thomas Potts, led the congregation to build a one-room stone chapel at the corner of Bellevue and Erskine Avenues. The first service was held on July 12, 1903 with Bellevue's first pastor, Dr. Henry Hurt. Thirty-two founding members signed the official charter on August 9, 1903. The church completed a 3,000 seat building in 1952, which was one of the first air-conditioned churches in Memphis. Bellevue became one of the largest Southern Baptist churches in the United States in the 1950s with more than 9,000 members. The church relocated to its current building (2000 Appling Road), which seats 7,000, on a 377-acre campus in Cordova, a Memphis suburb, in 1989. Bellevue is ranked 80th in the largest and fasting growing churches in America by LifeWay Research for Outreach Magazine.

Brainerd Baptist Church	Chattanooga	TN	1,899
Brentwood Baptist Church	Brentwood	TN	5,510
Cedar Springs Presbyterian	Knoxville	TN	3,700
Central Baptist Church	Knoxville	TN	4,213
Christ United Methodist	Memphis	TN	6,909
Christ United Methodist	Chattanooga	TN	4,100
ClearView Baptist Church	Franklin	TN	1,304
Cleveland First Baptist	Cleveland	TN	2,965
Cokesbury United Methodist	Knoxville	TN	4,454
Collierville First Baptist	Collierville	TN	1,390
Columbia First Baptist	Columbia	TN	1,064
Concord First Baptist	Knoxville	TN	2,846
Corryton Baptist Church	Corryton	TN	1,077

Dallas Bay Baptist Church	Hixson	TN	1,915
Englewood Baptist Church	Jackson	TN	2,556
Fairview Baptist Church	Corryton	TN	1,450
Faith Baptist Church	Bartlett	TN	1,583
Faith Promise Church	Knoxville	TN	4,355
Fellowship Bible Church	Brentwood	TN	6,000
First Baptist Concord	Knoxville	TN	8,000
First Presbyterian Church	Chattanooga	TN	2,500
Forest Hills Baptist	Nashville	TN	1,074

Germantown Baptist Germantown TN 12,000

The church was founded circa 1835, and it was officially recognized in 1838 as New Hope Baptist Church. The name was changed to Baptist Church at Germantown in 1841, the same year that the town received its charter and official name. Two decades later the church was burned during the Civil War, with only the pulpit Bible surviving the blaze. Faithful and resilient members presided over the rebuilding of the church on its original site. The white chapel served as the worship sanctuary until 1971.

As the town of Germantown experienced growth in the 1960's and 1970's, so did Germantown Baptist. Membership increased, ministries expanded and a new sanctuary was built to accommodate the growing church. Her influence and footprint in the local community were easily recognizable. Unprecedented growth in the 1980's necessitated a search for a larger property to house the expanding congregation and exploding ministries. Men of faith purchased the current property in 1987, and they held the property until the church could assume the mortgage. The new location and worship center were occupied and dedicated in 1995. Through the years, the congregation has responded to the needs of her members and the community at large. A recreation building was added to provide a home for indoor recreation and Student Ministry. The Faith building was added to provide a space for fellowship, dining, equipping and worship.

The most recent chapter of history at GBC began in 2010. The church called Pastor Charles Fowler to lead and guide her into the future. While Germantown Baptist has a robust lineage of faith and faithfulness, the vision for the future is greater still. Today, under the leadership of our Lord and our Pastor, GBC is deeply committed to being a disciple making church.

The gospel has shaped the history and ministry of Germantown Baptist and will continue to find faithful expression through future ministries.

The new campus is a 64 acres campus that includes a 3,000 seat sanctuary, two class-room buildings, a recreation complex with two basketball courts, a game room, a weight room, running track and racquetball courts, called the CORE, a dining room and coffee shop, a book store, library, music theater, baseball fields and nearby soccer fields, and a multimedia conference center.

Grace Baptist Church	Knoxville	TN	5,800
Grace Community Church	Clarksville	TN	2,030
Hendersonville First Baptist	Hendersonville	TN	2,775
Hermitage Hills Baptist	Hermitage	TN	1,080
Higher Ground Baptist	Kingsport	TN	1,254
Hillcrest Baptist Church	Lebanon	TN	1,200
Hilldale Baptist Church	Clarksville	TN	1,288
Hope Presbyterian Church	Cordova	TN	6,978
Immanuel Baptist Church	Lebanon	TN	1,136
Independent Presbyterian	Memphis	TN	2,500
Journey Church	Franklin	TN	1,000
Kirby Woods Baptist	Memphis	TN	1,250
LifePoint Church	Smyrna	TN	2,746
Long Hollow Baptist	Hendersonville	TN	7,154
Millington First Baptist	Millington	TN	1,330
Morristown First Baptist	Morristown	TN	1,350

Mount Zion Baptist Church Nashville TN 22,000

Mount Zion Baptist Church is one of the oldest black churches organized in Nashville, TN. The church was organized in 1866; just three years after President Lincoln had issued the Emancipation Proclamation. Throughout its rich history, Mount Zion was led by 14 dynamic pastors who preceded Bishop Joseph Walker, III. Mount Zion extended a call to its youngest son in ministry, Pastor Joseph W. Walker, III in April 1992, at 24-years-of-age. Before accepting the position as pastor, he served as the associate minister under Reverend Roberson. Pastor Walker had a vision of growth through studying God's Word. He was immediately embraced by the congregation. Bishop Walker is a native of Shreveport, Louisiana.

He began his pastorate in the spring of 1992 with 175 members. Presently, the ministry has grown to over 22,000 and continues to grow at a phenomenal rate of over 1,800 souls per year. Mount Zion has grown to eight weekly services in three locations. Under Bishop Walker's leadership, the church engaged in the completion of a $17 million dollar, state-of-the-art ministry complex that seats 5,000 which was completed in October 2001. This is the first phase of a $60 million dollar, twelve-year project.

In December 2003, Mount Zion completed a third location in Antioch, TN. This $7 million dollar retail center and ministry complex includes a children's wing and serves as a multi-purpose facility that seats 2,000.

Bishop Walker currently serves as International Presiding Bishop-Elect for the Full Gospel Baptist Church Fellowship under the leadership of International Presiding Bishop Paul S. Morton, Sr. for five years, Bishop Walker served as the Bishop of Evangelism. At age 41, Bishop Walker has many academic accomplishments, including a Bachelor of Arts from Southern University; A Master's of Divinity from Vanderbilt University; and a Doctorate of Ministry from Princeton Theological Seminary, all with honors.

Mount Zion Baptist	Whites Creek	TN	9,000
New Vision Baptist	Murfreesboro	TN	3,250
Overcoming Believers	Knoxville	TN	2,500
Powell First Baptist Church	Powell	TN	1,356
Sevier Heights Baptist	Knoxville	TN	3,464
Sevierville First	Sevierville	TN	1,923
Silverdale Baptist Church	Chattanooga	TN	2,584
Stevens Street Baptist	Cookeville	TN	1,275
Stuart Heights Baptist	Hixson	TN	1,161

Temple Baptist Church	Powell	TN	6,000
The Glade Church	Gladeville	TN	1,197
The River Community	Cookeville	TN	1,096
Thompson Station Baptist	Thompson S	TN	2,041
Tulip Grove Baptist Church	Old Hickory	TN	1,000
Wallace Memorial Baptist	Knoxville	TN	2,059
West Jackson Baptist	Jackson	TN	1,047

Woodland Park Baptist   Chattanooga TN 1,120

April 26, 1914, Woodland Park Baptist Church, with twenty six adults and one youth, was organized. Little did this small group know God's plan for this church, and the door of witness that it would become.

By 1946 the membership had grown to 2,392 and in that year there were 380 additions with more than half of them coming by profession of faith and desiring to be baptized.

Woodland Park has a great desire to be a part of reaching the world for Christ by joining hands with the International Mission Board, and by financially supporting missionaries and mission agencies to see this task accomplished. The extended missionary family and those receiving financial and prayer support has grown to 90+ missionaries in approximately 35 countries.

Texas

121 Community Church   Grapevine   TX 1,440

121 Community Church was started in the fall of 1999 when a group of 23 people met for the first time after much prayer and conversation. They firmly believed that this was God's idea, and boldly acted upon that belief. The first worship service took place in one of the families' homes in Colleyville that September.

121 Community Church has been, and will continue to be, a church with Christ at the center, under the authority of His Word. It is a home where people's lives have been transformed; allowing them to tackle personal challenges and understanding their significance within His plan. And we are a church where children, students, and adults are daily seeking God in His Word, authentically investing in one another in community through LifeGroups, worshiping with freedom, serving others, and communicating the story of Christ locally, nationally, and globally.

Abundant Living Faith	El Paso	TX	12,400
Alamo City Christian	San Antonio	TX	2,125
Antioch Community	Waco	TX	4,000
Bannockburn Baptist	Austin	TX	1,564
Baptist Temple	McAllen	TX	2,000
Bay Area Fellowship	Corpus Christi	TX	6,957
Bear Creek Baptist Church	Katy	TX	2,968
Beltway Park Baptist	Abilene	TX	3,067
Birchman Baptist Church	Fort Worth	TX	1,470
Brentwood Baptist Church	Houston	TX	1,547
Calvary Baptist Church	Beaumont	TX	1,959
Cathedral of Hope	Dallas	TX	4,834
Central Baptist Church,	College Station	TX	3,000
Champion Forest Baptist	Houston	TX	5,456
Christ United Methodist	Plano	TX	6,200
Clear Creek Community	League City	TX	4,322
Coggin Avenue Baptist	Brownwood	TX	1,024

Community Bible San Antonio TX 14,031

Mission Statement To Reach, Teach, and Help People in Jesus' Name. History Community Bible Church began on May 26, 1990 meeting in a conference room of a local hotel. From day one the mission of CBC has always been to reach people with the good news of salvation in Jesus' name, to teach people how to live the Christian life according to the Bible, and to help people through the hard times in life.

Community Life Church	Forney	TX	1,876
Community of Faith	Houston	TX	6,000
Concord Missionary Baptist	Dallas	TX	1,400
Concordia Lutheran	San Antonio	TX	7,300

Cornerstone Church San Antonio TX 8,400

Cornerstone Church is a mega church located in San Antonio, TX. Our church was founded in 1975 and is Non-Denominational / Independent. Cornerstone Church offers

3 weekend worship services. Leaders: John C. Hagee, Founder and Senior Pastor. Matthew Hagee, Executive Pastor.

Coronado Baptist Church	El Paso	TX	1,000
Cottonwood Creek Baptist	Allen	TX	1,772
Covenant Church	Carrollton	TX	8,000
Cowboy Church	Waxahachie	TX	1,632
Crestview Baptist Church	Georgetown	TX	1,300
Cross Brand Cowboy	Tyler	TX	1,100
Crosspoint Church	Pearland	TX	1,000
Crossroads Baptist	Woodlands	TX	1,092
Custer Road U Methodist	Plano	TX	6,411
Del Sol Church	El Paso	TX	1,289
Denton Bible Church	Denton	TX	3,000
Fallbrook Baptist Church	Houston	TX	5,500

Largest Churches In The United States

Fellowship Church Grapevine, Tx 18,355

Fellowship Church is tied to the Southern Baptist Convention in a very loose way, opting not to emphasize its connection in order to avoid scaring off new converts who might be uncomfortable with the SBC label. It began in 1989 as an offshoot of First Baptist Church of Irving, Texas, but a name change and more people-oriented services led to quick and steady growth.

Fellowship of the Parks	Keller	TX	1,896
Fielder Road Baptist	Arlington	TX	2,312
First Baptist Church	Pasadena	TX	4,250
First Baptist Church	Dallas	TX	3,426
First Baptist Church	Arlington	TX	2,401
First Baptist Church	Wichita Falls	TX	2,182
First Baptist Church	Amarillo	TX	2,100
First Baptist Church	Rockwall	TX	1,850
First Baptist Church	Midland	TX	1,700
First Baptist Church	Texarkana	TX	1,600

First Baptist Church	Garland	TX	1,517
First Baptist Church	Denton	TX	1,495
First Baptist Church	San Antonio	TX	1,437
First Baptist Church	Carrollton	TX	1,354
First Baptist Church	Universal Cty	TX	1,252
First Baptist Church	Lubbock	TX	1,234
First Baptist Church	Midlothian	TX	1,202
First Baptist Church	Lewisville	TX	1,183
First Baptist Church	Hurst	TX	1,150
First Baptist Church	Odessa	TX	1,145
First Baptist Church	Burleson	TX	1,125
First Baptist Church	The Woodlands	TX	1,105
First Baptist Church	Irving	TX	1,100
First Baptist Church	Richardson	TX	1,100
First Baptist Church	Georgetown	TX	1,061
First Baptist Church	Colleyville	TX	1,034
First Baptist Church	Belton	TX	1,025
First Baptist Church	Pflugerville	TX	1,000
First Baptist Church	Dallas	TX	12,000
First Baptist Church	Houston	TX	6,458
First Baptist Church	Allen	TX	1,334
First Baptist Church	Frisco	TX	1,223
First Baptist Church	McKinney	TX	2,036
First Baptist Church	Wylie	TX	2,200
First Baptist Church	Woodway	TX	2,100
First Baptist Church,	Euless	TX	2,534
First Baptist Forney	Forney	TX	2,000
First Keller	Keller	TX	1,200
First Presbyterian	Houston	TX	3,600
First St. John M.Baptist	Fort Worth	TX	1,400
Fountain of Praise	Houston	TX	11,800
Friendship Baptist Church	The Colony	TX	1,075
Friendship West Baptist	Dallas	TX	8,000

Gateway Church Southlake TX 27,000

Gateway Church is a non-denominational Evangelical Charismatic Christian church located in Southlake, Texas. In 2015, *Outreach* magazine named Gateway as the 4th largest church in the US. The church estimates it has 36,000 active members. In 2014, the church averaged 27,271 weekly attendees, with 50,605 attending over Easter weekend, a total of 3,528 professions of faith, and 1,772 water baptisms. The church is home to the Christian recording artist and Dove Award winner Kari Jobe, who works as a worship pastor.

On September 16, 1999, Pastor Robert Morris began to plan a Bible-based, evangelistic church in Southlake, Texas. Morris hoped to serve Northeast Tarrant County, the

Dallas/Fort Worth Metroplex and beyond. Gateway's first service was on Easter morning, April 23, 2000, at the Hilton Hotel in Grapevine with approximately 180 people in attendance. A few weeks later, the church began meeting on Saturday nights at Christ Our King Church in Southlake. In July 2001, Gateway Church began meeting at the A World of Learning daycare facility in Grapevine, during which time the church grew to five services with over 2,000 people attending weekly.

Robert Morris is featured on the weekly television program, The Blessed Life, produced by the church. He is the author of 11 books including *The Blessed Life, From Dream to Destiny, The Power of Your Words, The God I Never Knew* and *The Blessed Church*. Morris is also part of the advisory counsel for The Vernon Wells Perfect 10 Foundation.[7] He is also the Chairman of Board of The King's University, an Overseer of New Life Church in Colorado Springs and an Apostolic Elder of Trinity Fellowship Church in Amarillo, Texas. He holds an honorary Doctorate of Letters from the King's University.

We're excited to announce Gateway's new Dallas Campus! We recently purchased the campus from Prestonwood Baptist Church and are looking forward to being able to connect with the Dallas community in 2016

Church	City	State	Number
Glenview Baptist Church	Fort Worth	TX	2,280
Good Hope M Baptist	Houston	TX	1,355
Grace Fellowship Church	Paradise	TX	1,377
Grace Point Church	San Antonio	TX	1,500
Great Commission Baptist	Fort Worth	TX	2,453
Greater Cornerstone Bapt.	Dallas	TX	4,250
Greater St Matthew Bapt.	Houston	TX	1,400
Green Acres Baptist Church	Tyler	TX	5,056
Harris Creek Baptist	McGregor	TX	1,350
Harvest Baptist Church	Watauga	TX	1,132
Higher Dimension Baptist	Houston	TX	9,000
Highland Baptist Church	Waco	TX	1,064
Hillcrest Baptist Church	Cedar Hill	TX	1,008
Hillside Christian Church	Amarillo	TX	7,000
Houston Northwest Baptist	Houston	TX	1,266
Houston's First Baptist	Houston	TX	5,607
Humble Area's First Baptist	Humble	TX	1,788
Hunters Glen Baptist	Plano	TX	1,150
Hyde Park Baptist Church	Austin	TX	1,859
Iglesia Bautista	W Brownsville	TX	1,750
Inspiring Body of Christ	Dallas	TX	7,500
Keystone Church	Keller	TX	1,422
Kingsland Baptist Church	Katy	TX	2,408
Lake Pointe Church	Rockwall	TX	11,225
Lakeside Baptist Church	Granbury	TX	1,287

Lakewood Church Houston, Texas 43,500

Lakewood Church is a nondenominational charismatic Christian megachurch located in Houston, Texas. It is the largest congregation in the United States, averaging more than 43,500 in attendance per week/ The 16,800-seat Lakewood Church Central Campus, home to four English language services and two Spanish language services per week,[ ]is located at the former Compaq Center. Joel Osteen is the senior pastor of Lakewood Church with his wife, Victoria, who serves as co-pastor. Lakewood Church is a part of the Word of Faith movement.

Even compared with the other churches on this list, Lakewood is a behemoth, packing more than 40,000 people into what used to be the Compaq Center, formerly the Summit arena home of the Houston Rockets. The evangelical congregation is nondenominational, and weekly services are broadcast in local markets nationwide as well as on the Trinity Broadcasting Network.

Church	City	State	Number
Mesquite Friendship Baptist	Mesquite	TX	1,420
Metropolitan Baptist	Houston	TX	3,439
Mims Baptist Church	Conroe	TX	1,100
Mobberly Baptist Church	Longview	TX	2,313
Mt Hebron Missionary Baptist	Garland	TX	1,051
New Beginnings Baptist	Longview	TX	2,000
New Faith Church	Houston	TX	2,500
New Light Christian Ctr	Houston	TX	20,000
New Song Church	Carrollton	TX	1,050
N Richland Hills Baptist	N Richland Hills	TX	1,517
North Side Baptist	Weatherford	TX	1,135
Northside Christian	Spring	TX	2,000
Northwood Church	Keller	TX	1,913
Oak Hills Church	San Antonio	TX	9,500
Oakwood Baptist Church	New Braunfels	TX	2,947
Paramount Baptist Church	Amarillo	TX	1,372
Park Cities Baptist Church	Dallas	TX	2,340
Park Cities Presbyterian	Dallas	TX	5,500
Parkway Church	Victoria	TX	1,215
PaulAnn Baptist Church	San Angelo	TX	1,843
Pioneer Drive Baptist	Abilene	TX	1,025
Prestonwood Baptist	Plano	TX	5,815
Redeemer Church	Lubbock	TX	1,150
Resurrection Baptist	Schertz	TX	1,350
Riverbend Baptist Church	Austin	TX	3,500
Rockpointe Church	Flower Mound	TX	1,500
Sagemont Church	Houston	TX	4,136

Second Baptist Church Houston, Texas **26,022**

The Young family is famous in megachurch circles: Ed Young, Sr. heads up Houston's Second Baptist Church, while his son oversees Grapevine's Fellowship Church. Second Baptist has five locations around the city to help reach more worshippers, with numerous groups that meet throughout the week to connect with people on a more intimate level.

Second Baptist Church Houston is a megachurch in Houston, Texas, USA affiliated with the Southern Baptist Convention that has a membership of over 63,000. Its senior pastor is Dr. Ed Young. Second Baptist Church is aligned with the Southern Baptists of Texas Convention, which broke away from the Baptist General Convention of

Texas in 1998. A 2008 survey by Outreach magazine gave attendance at 23,659. In 2009 average weekly attendance was 22,723, making it the largest Baptist church in the country and the 5th largest church.

The church was founded in 1927. In 1946 the church sponsored foundation of the Second Baptist School as a self-supporting agency. The school occupies a 42-acre campus in the Memorial area and is open to students without regard to race, religion, or economic background. In 1957, Second Baptist moved west to the current main location at 6400 Woodway Drive in Houston. The Woodway church boasts a pipe organ with 192 stops and 10,412 total pipes, one of the largest in the world.

In 1979 the church launched a weekly broadcast of worship services on local television. In 1982 a local radio program began, as well as national TV broadcasting. Since then this has expanded into international television, radio and internet distribution of the church's message.[The church participates in the *Faith Comes By Hearing* Audio Bible listening program.

Second Baptist Church	Baytown	TX	1,100
Seoul Baptist Church	Houston	TX	1,931
Shoreline Christian Center	Austin	TX	8,000
Silverlake Church	Pearland	TX	2,766
Southcliff Baptist Church	Fort Worth	TX	1,057
Southcrest Baptist Church	Lubbock	TX	1,833
Southwest Community Baptist	Houston	TX	3,400

Spring Baptist Church	Spring	TX	1,390
St Luke Missionary Baptist	Humble	TX	1,045
St. John Baptist Church	Grand Prairie	TX	8,200
St. Martin's Episcopal	Houston	TX	8,311
Stonebriar Community	Frisco	TX	5,200
StoneBridge Church	The Woodlands	TX	1,200
Stonegate Fellowship	Midland	TX	1,600
Sugar Creek Baptist Church	Sugar Land	TX	3,790
Sunnyvale First Baptist	Sunnyvale	TX	1,500
Tallowood Baptist Church	Houston	TX	1,907
The Austin Stone Com.	Austin	TX	6,336
The Avenue Church	Waxahachie	TX	2,044
The Church Without Walls	Houston	TX	6,411
The Connection Church	Kyle	TX	1,100
The Fellowship At Cinco Ranch	Katy	TX	1,038
The Fort Bend Church	Sugar Land	TX	2,189
The Fountain of Praise	Houston	TX	9,000
The Heights Baptist Church	Richardson	TX	2,866
The Potter's House	Dallas	TX	16,140
The Village Church	Highland Village	TX	10,156
The Village Church	Flower Mound	TX	10,030
The Woodlands United Methodist	Woodlands	TX	18,500
Travis Avenue Baptist	Fort Worth	TX	1,346
Valley Creek Baptist	Flower Mound	TX	1,400
Walnut Ridge Baptist	Mansfield	TX	1,140
West University Baptist	Houston	TX	1,178
Westside Baptist Church	Lewisville	TX	1,100
Willow Park Baptist	Aledo	TX	1,016
Windsor Village U Methodist	Houston	TX	17,045

Woodlands Church The Woodlands, Tx 18,385

Woodlands Church, led by Senior Pastor Kerry Shook, is a non-denominational church in the Houston, TX area. Woodlands Church is one church in many locations with our main campus in The Woodlands, TX, and several satellite campuses including a Church Online Internet campus. We want to personally invite you to experience a warm and friendly church home. The service is relaxed, the message is relevant and the atmosphere is amazing! We have quality events and programs for you and your entire family.

Located in a suburb outside Houston, Woodlands Church was founded by Pastor Kerry Shook in 1993 and has since grown to be one of the biggest in the nation. The main campus in The Woodlands also supports three other campuses in the outlying Houston region. There's also an "online campus" for people to stream sermons and worship services.

Utah

South Mountain Community Draper UT 1800

SMCC is a non-denominational Christian church, meeting at many locations in Utah—Draper, South Jordan and West Jordan in the Salt Lake City area, and campuses in Lehi and St. George. You will experience joyful worship music and hope-filled biblical messages. Your children will have fun while learning about our loving God in a safe environment.

Iglesia Rios de Agua Via   Ogden   UT 2000

Rivers of Living Water is a Pentecostal/ Apostolic congregation and is a Spanish speaking church.

Washington Heights Baptist Ogden UT 2200

We are an Independent Baptist Church that has been in existence since 1957. We are part of the Ohio Association of Regular Baptist Churches which is a home for independent, autonomous Baptist churches who desire like-minded fellowship. At Washington Heights we want to provide a place for you no matter what your need may be; a place to worship and learn in our Celebration Services, a place to connect in our Adult Bible Fellowships, and a place to serve in our variety of ministries.

Virginia

Bon Air Baptist Church	Richmond	VA	1,440
Bonsack Baptist Church	Roanoke	VA	1,000
Calvary Revival Church	Norfolk	VA	7,000
Colonial Heights Baptist	Colonial Hts	VA	5,200
Columbia Baptist Church	Falls Church	VA	1,319
Cool Spring Baptist	Mechanicsvile	VA	1,100
Deep Creek Baptist Church	Chesapeake	VA	1,061
Fairfax Community Church	Fairfax	VA	2,000

Faith Landmarks Ministries Richmond VA 10,000

Easter Sunday (April 6, 1980) marked the very first service of Faith Landmarks Ministries (FLM) (though at this time, the church had no name). There were 13 people in attendance.

God has given a five-fold vision to Pastors Randy and Cherie Gilbert for Faith Landmarks Ministries. This vision is implemented throughout each department and element of FLM. We want to see God's people discipled and ministered to on a deeper level, and give non-believers access to a ministry that has a heart to connect them with a loving Savior who can change their lives and their future forever. This **vision** provides:

- →WORSHIP to help you focus on God
- →FELLOWSHIP to help you face life's challenges
- →DISCIPLESHIP to help fortify your faith
- →MINISTRY OPPORTUNITIES to help fulfil your purpose
- →EVANGELISM to help fulfil our mission

Fellowship Community	Salem	VA	1,305
First Baptist Church	Roanoke	VA	1,266
First Baptist Church	Richmond	VA	1,030
First Baptist Church	Norfolk	VA	2,402
First Baptist Church	Alexandria	VA	1,067
First Baptist Church	Woodbridge	VA	1,349
Franklin Heights Baptist	Rocky Mount	VA	1,256
Grove Avenue Baptist	Richmond	VA	1,151
Highlands Fellowship	Abingdon	VA	4,000
Hyland Heights Baptist	Lynchburg	VA	1,314
Korean Central Presbyterian	Centreville	VA	4,500
Liberty Baptist Church	Hampton	VA	4,014
Lifepoint Church	Fredericksburg	VA	2,643
London Bridge Baptist	Virginia Beach	VA	1,010

McLean Bible Church McLean VA 16,500

McLean Bible Church, which was founded in 1961 by five families in Northern Virginia, is a non-denominational, evangelical Christian megachurch with multiple locations in the Washington, DC metropolitan area. Lon Solomon, a Jewish convert to Christianity, has been MBC's senior pastor since 1980. Solomon also serves on the board of directors of Jews for Jesus and was appointed by President George W. Bush to the President's Committee for Intellectual Disabilities. An average of 13,000 adults attend each weekend at the church's several campuses. Its current service locations are Arlington, Montgomery County, Loudoun, Prince William, and Tysons. The church offers live webcasts of its Sunday services.

Mount Ararat Baptist   Stafford   VA   1,705
Mount Pleasant Baptist   Herndon   VA   1,250
Powhatan Community   Powhatan   VA   1,200
Richmond Outreach Center Richmond   VA   4,000
River Oak Church   Chesapeake   VA   1,890
Spotswood Baptist Church Fredericksburg VA   1,908
St. Paul's Baptist Church   Richmond   VA   6,488
The Heights Baptist Church Colonial Hts   VA   2,225

Thomas Road Baptist Lynchburg VA 8,350

On June 17, 1956, 35 adults and their children gathered in the Mountain View Elementary School in Lynchburg, Virginia for the church's first Sunday worship service. That week, leaders of the church and a particularly aggressive young man named Jerry Falwell, the church's founding pastor, searched for a place to house their new church.

On May 15, 2007, Dr. Jerry Falwell finished his work on this earth and went home to his Heavenly Father. As the new pastor, Dr. Falwell's son Jonathan is continuing the vision and legacy put forth by his father.

Under Jonathan Falwell's leadership the church has experienced phenomenal growth. Every month, hundreds of people make the decision to accept Christ as Savior and thousands have joined our church body.

Vienna Presbyterian   Vienna   VA   2,500
Virginia Highlands Christian Abingdon   VA   3,583
Water's Edge Church   Yorktown   VA   3,432

Washington

Champions Centre   Tacoma   WA   6,500

Christian Faith Center Federal Way WA 10,000

On January 6, 1980, Casey and Wendy founded Christian Faith Center and began pastoring a group of 30. They were ordained in July 1980 by Dr. Fred Price at Crenshaw Christian Center in Los Angeles, California.

Christian Faith Center Core Values
1. Salvation & Discipleship
2. Worship & Word
3. Families & Culture
4. Serving & Giving
5. Worldwide Outreach

On a weekly basis they have over 150 nations represented in our congregation.

Cornwall Church	Bellingham	WA	2,500
Crossroads Community	Vancouver	WA	6,000
Life Center Foursquare	Spokane	WA	5,000
Living Hope Church	Vancouver	WA	6,000
Overlake Christian Church	Redmond	WA	3,000
Tacoma First Baptist	Tacoma	WA	1,200
The City Church	Kirkland	WA	7,155
University Presbyterian	Seattle	WA	4,000
Christ the King	Bellingham	WA	4000
Westgate Chapel	Edmonds	WA	2000
Overlake Christian	Redmond	WA	3000
First Presbyterian	Bellevue	WA	2203
Calvary Community	Sumner	WA	3000
Puyallup Foursquare	Puyallup	WA	3500

Christian Faith Seattle WA 8000

Christian Faith Center Today Christian Faith Center, pastored by Pastors Casey & Wendy Treat, consists of two major church campuses in Federal Way and Mill Creek, WA, a network of Connect Groups, Vision College, and Christian Faith School. At Christian Faith Center, our ongoing vision is to Pastor the Northwest, Teach the Nation, and Inspire the World, and part of our vision for growth is reflected in the continued expansion of our facilities. The rapid growth of our church over the last 25 years has given us the enviable problem of having to accommodate the number of people attending our church and schools.

In their last two years of Bible College, Casey and Wendy Treat began to sense the call of God on their lives to plant a church. On January 6, 1980, Casey and Wendy founded Christian Faith Center and began pastoring a group of 30. They were ordained in July 1980 by Dr. Fred Price at

Crenshaw Christian Center in Los Angeles, California.

In 1984, Casey and Wendy founded Christian Faith School (for pre-school through 12th grade), and later Vision College.

With the first annual Vision Spiritual Life Conference in 1985, Casey and Wendy launched Vision Ministry Fellowship. This organization provides support for men and women in leadership who want to grow and more fully develop themselves and their ministries through teaching, mentoring, and relationship building. Casey and Wendy Treat have been instrumental in helping to plant and support numerous churches through this ministry. CFC North in Everett Washington was launched in July 2003.

In 2010, Christian Faith Center started claiming to be the largest church in the Pacific Northwest, with two locations (Federal Way and Mill Creek) claiming more than 10,000 people attending weekly services.

Mars Hill Church	Seattle	WA	13109
Westminster Chapel	Bellevue	WA	3000
Church For All Nations	Tacoma	WA	2000
First Presbyterian Church	Spokane	WA	2500
Eastridge Church	Issaquah	WA	1900
New Life Foursquare h	Everett	WA	2700
Saint John Baptist Church	Tacoma	WA	2000
New Life Fellowship	Bothell	WA	3000
Calvary Fellowship	Mlake Terr	WA	1900

Bethany Community	Seattle	WA	2874
Mount Zion Baptist	Seattle	WA	2500
Canyon Hills Community	Bothell	WA	2100
Life Center	Tacoma	WA	4811
Gold Creek Community	Mill Creek	WA	2389
Eastside Foursquare	Bothell	WA	2300
Tabernacle Miss Baptist	Seattle	WA	1800
Cascade Community	Monroe	WA	2000
Champions Centre	Tacoma	WA	5500
Northshore Baptist	Kirkland	WA	2400
Church of Living Water	Olympia	WA	2100
Cornwall Church	Bellingham	WA	2300
Seventh-day Adventist	Walla Walla	WA	1800
East Lake Community	Bothell	WA	4500
New Heights Church	Vancouver	WA	4000
NewLife Church	Silverdale	WA	3044

Christ the King Burlington WA   17000

Our Vision is to see a prevailing, multi-location church emerge that will transform the spiritual landscape.

This church will convene in hundreds of small groups, with worship centers strategically located in every community.

We've got a casual atmosphere and a growing group of loving people who find ways to support each other in "doing life" together. We make sure that our teaching is relevant and applicable to living our lives out each day. We especially welcome people who have given up on church in the past but are interested in giving a relationship with God another try.

Calvary Chapel	Spokane	WA	2600
New Life Church	Renton	WA	2733
Grace Community Church	Auburn	WA	2000
Washington Cathedral	Redmond	WA	2000
River of Life Fellowship	Kent	WA	2000
The City Church	Kirkland	WA	6300
Centro Cristiano Ministries	Manson	WA	2000
Antioch Bible Church	Redmond	WA	3500
Bethel Church	Richland	WA	2400
N County Christ the King	Lynden	WA	1950
University Presbyterian	Seattle	WA	3896
Crossroads Community	Vancouver	WA	4000
Lighthouse Christian	Puyallup	WA	1800
Life Center Foursquare	Spokane	WA	4500
Living Hope	Vancouver	WA	5200
Crossroads Bible Church	Bellevue	WA	2100
Northwest Church	Federal Way	WA	1800
Christ Memorial Church	Poulsbo	WA	2000

Wisconsin

Elmbrook Church   Brookfield   WI   7,013

It all began in 1957 - Five families began praying that God would do something big in their community. They didn't have a pastor, and they didn't have a building...they just prayed.

Pretty soon, there were 30 people meeting at Leland school in Elm Grove. They called themselves the First Baptist Church of Brookfield.

It turns out God DID want to do something big...In 1970, Stuart Briscoe was called as Senior Pastor of the renamed

"Elmbrook Church", and there were 450+ meeting in two services.

Hales Corners Lutheran	Hales Corners	WI	8,577
Jacob's Well	Eau Claire	WI	1,590
Christian Faith Fellowship	Milwaukee	WI	6000
Bethel Lutheran Church	Madison	WI	1800
Appleton Alliance Church	Appleton	WI	3000
Eastbrook Church	Milwaukee	WI	2000
Blackhawk Church	Verona	WI	4000
Christ the Rock Community	Menasha	WI	3000
Fox River Christian	Waukesha	WI	2400
Celebration Ch - Bayside	Green Bay	WI	4000
Alliance Missionary Church	Marshfield	WI	1800
Door Creek Church	Madison	WI	2000
Central Christian Church	Beloit	WI	1981
Oak Creek Assembly of God	Oak Creek	WI	2229
Journey Church	Kenosha	WI	2400

West Virginia

Chestnut Ridge	Morgantown	WV	2,400
Bible Center Church	Charleston	WV	2500

Maranatha Fellowship Saint Albans WV 2200

Maranatha Fellowship is a loving, caring, congregation of people who come from every walk of life. Our main purpose is to share the good news of Jesus and to help individuals find fulfilment in the Lord's will for their life. We have found that serving Jesus is thrills, romance, and adventure.

The St. Albans Campus has 3 power packed services on Sundays. We have one at 9:00AM, one at 10:45AM, and one at 6:30PM.

Wyoming

Highland Park Community Casper WY 2500

God led a handful of believers and a bi-vocational pastor in 1952 to begin a house church. Two years later construction began on a building at 955 South Washington, and we became The First Church of God. By faith and the labor of willing volunteers, the church was completed and God filled the building with people.

The dream continued and faith expanded when the small church stepped out again in 1975 to relocate to 12th and Missouri. Upon completion three years later, we took the name of the community we hoped to serve, and became known as The Highland Park Community Church.

As the congregation continued to thrive, the building was expanded several times until space limitations necessitated another relocation, this time to the vacant

LaBelle's building on 2nd Street. God honored our faithfulness and continued to bring significant growth and impact, not only in Casper, but literally around the world.

Over the course of two decades that building was remodeled, completed and filled to accommodate four weekend worship services, vibrant children and youth ministries, a life-changing counseling center called The Healing Place, over 100 community groups for youth and adults, and a Faith Promise Missions outreach that spanned the globe.

But the story didn't stop there...

God brought us into a new house, the place we sit today, a house that HE built. But with this gift comes great responsibility. What now? How can we utilize this new "hub" to serve God? To serve others?

10 Biggest Churches in United States

Often meeting in stadiums or sprawling campuses, the biggest churches in the U.S. are known for their size, popular profile, and economic impact on the local community. They also reflect a growing diversity of people and worship methods, combining online resources and multiple locations to maximize their size. Here are the ten biggest churches at the end of 2009...

1. Lakewood Church
Location: Houston, Texas
Total attendance: 43,500
Pastor: Joel Osteen

Even compared with the other churches on this list, Lakewood is a behemoth, packing more than 40,000 people into what used to be the Compaq Center, formerly the Summit arena home of the Houston Rockets. The evangelical congregation is nondenominational, and weekly services are broadcast in local markets nationwide as well as on the Trinity Broadcasting Network.

2. LifeChurch.tv
Location: Based in Edmond, Oklahoma
Total attendance: 26,776
Pastor: Craig Groeschel

What began as a tiny congregation meeting in a garage in the mid-1990s has since become a multi-site church with a number of campuses that use satellite video to coordinate worship. There are now venues in Oklahoma, Texas, Tennessee, Florida, and New York, and services are also streamed online for people who wish to watch from home.

3. Willow Creek Community Church

Location: South Barrington, Illinois
Total attendance: 23,400
Pastor: Bill Hybels

Located in a suburb of Chicago, Willow Creek was the first church to deploy giant HD screens in its theater to aid those who can't quite see the action on stage. They've also got services across an array of locations in and around Chicago.

4. North Point Community Church

Location: Alpharetta, Georgia
Total attendance: 23,377
Pastor: Andy Stanley

Founded in 1995, North Point now utilizes three campuses for its weekly services. They've also planted more than 20 churches throughout the country and in Canada that serve their communities as partner churches with the flagship location in Alpharetta, a suburb of Atlanta.

5. Second Baptist Church

Location: Houston, Texas
Total attendance: 22,723
Pastor: Ed Young, Sr.

The Young family is famous in megachurch circles: Ed Young, Sr. heads up Houston's Second Baptist Church, while his son oversees Grapevine's Fellowship Church.

Second Baptist has five locations around the city to help reach more worshippers, with numerous groups that meet throughout the week to connect with people on a more intimate level.

6. Saddleback Church
Location: Lake Forest, California
Total attendance: 22,418
Pastor: Rick Warren

Saddleback Church, in Southern California's Orange County, is affiliated with the Southern Baptist Convention. Founded in 1980 by Rick Warren, the church is one of the most prominent evangelical bodies in the nation, and Warren is best known as the author of the 2002 devotional book *The Purpose-Driven Life.*

7. *Fellowship Church*

Location: Grapevine, Texas
Total attendance: 18,355
Pastor: Ed Young, Jr.

Fellowship Church is tied to the Southern Baptist Convention in a very loose way, opting not to emphasize its connection in order to avoid scaring off new converts who might be uncomfortable with the SBC label. It began in 1989 as an offshoot of First Baptist Church of Irving, Texas, but a name change and more people-oriented services led to quick and steady growth.

8. Southeast Christian Church
Location: Louisville, Kentucky
Total attendance: 17,261
Pastor: Dave Stone

This 17,000-strong congregation in Kentucky is affiliated with the Independent Christian Churches/Churches of Christ, which differ from other autonomous Churches of Christ in the use of instrumental worship music. The church has been growing since its founding in 1962, and in 2009 opened a satellite campus in Jeffersonville, Indiana.

9. <u>Woodlands Church</u>
Location: The Woodlands, Texas
Total attendance: 17,142
Pastor: Kerry Shook

Located in a suburb outside Houston, Woodlands Church was founded by Pastor Kerry Shook in 1993 and has since grown to be one of the biggest in the nation. The main campus in The Woodlands also supports three other campuses in the outlying Houston region. There's also an "online campus" for people to stream sermons and worship services.

10. <u>Calvary Chapel Fort Lauderdale</u>
Location: Fort Lauderdale, Florida
Total attendance: 15,921
Pastor: Bob Coy

The biggest megachurch in Florida has been going strong for 25 years under the direction of Bob Coy. In addition to a thriving variety of small groups for people of all ages, the church's site archives worship services for streaming or download.

Riches Ministers in the United States

The following ministers were recently reported by ETINSIDE ONLINE Magazine. The following comments are theirs.

It might be argued that the reason why ministers are more likely to make money today is because they utilize more money making opportunities such as writing books, producing movies and speaking engagements.

Some of which make enough to have private planes (Eddie Long) refurbished arenas as churches (Joel Osteen) and flourishing press houses (Rick Warren).

There will be many who will say that these pastors shouldn't be making this much money. Before you judge, keep in mind that the average yearly household salary in The Democratic Republic of Congo in Africa is $422, so they could be saying the same about you!

This article is not to bash anyone, but here are men and women who inspire others while achieving their dreams.

1. Kenneth Copeland

Net Worth $760 Million

He runs Kenneth Copeland Ministries. His ministry's 1,500-acre campus is a half-hour drive from Fort Worth includes a church, a private airstrip, a hangar for the ministry's $17.5 million jet and other aircraft, and a $6 million church owned lakefront mansion. He is very close to being a Billionaire even though he already claims billion dollar status.

2. Pat Robertson

Net Worth $100 Million

Pat Robertson launched the Christian Broadcasting Network in Virginia, and the network is now broadcast in 180 countries. In the late 80s, he ran for President, but was unsuccessful. He runs a number of large companies, including the Christian Coalition, a Christian Right organization that exists to raise monetary and public support for conservative political candidates.

3. Benny Hinn

Net Worth $42 Million

Israeli televangelist, Benny Hinn is best known for his regular "Miracle

Crusades" – revival meeting/faith healing summits that are usually held in large stadiums in major cities, which are later broadcast worldwide on his television program, "This Is Your Day".

4. Joel Osteen

Net Worth $40 Million

Joel Osteen is an author, televangelist, and pastor of Lakewood Church in Houston, Texas. He took over his father's role as a pastor and televangelist, despite having very little formal religious training, in 1999. Since then, the Lakewood Church broadcast has grown exponentially and can be seen in 100 different countries.

5. Creflo Dollar

Net Worth $27 Million

American Bible teacher, pastor, and the founder of World Changers Church International, Creflo Dollar, is one of the most successful preachers in America.

6. Billy Graham
Net Worth $25 Million

Billy Graham is a Southern Baptist who rose to celebrity status as his sermons were broadcast on radio and television stations around the country. In 1950 he founded the Billy Graham Evangelistic Association in Minneapolis, Minnesota. Within a few years the civil rights movement began to sweep the nation. Billy, who had never really thought much about the plight of African Americans was instantly inspired to help the cause. He began refusing to speak or appear at events that were segregated. He joined the Montgomery Bus Boycott in 1955 where he met and befriended Martin Luther King, Jr. In 1957, Billy invited Dr. King to join him during a 16 week Christian event held at New York City's Madison Square Garden. This 16 week event attracted more than 2.3 million visitors from around the country and helped propel Dr. King and the Civil Rights movement into the mainstream conscience. Billy personally posted bail for Dr. King on several occasions after the MLK had been arrested during demonstrations. Billy Graham was also the official spiritual advisor to several Presidents including Nixon and Eisenhower. It has been estimated that during his lifetime, Billy's sermons have reached an audience across television and radio of more than 2.2 billion people. He married his wife Ruth in 1943 and they remained together until her death in 2007.

7. Rick Warren

Net Worth $25 Million

Rick Warren founded Saddleback Church in Lake Forest, California; it is now the country's eighth-largest church. Warren is the author of a handful of books, including "The Purpose Driven Church" and "The Purpose Driven Life". Warren believes in a five-point plan to bring global harmony to Earth; he calls it his "P.E.A.C.E. Plan". It calls for planting churches, equipping servant leaders, assisting the poor, caring for the sick, and education. He and his wife aim to live on ten percent of their income and donate the rest to charity.

8. Bishop T. D Jakes

Net Worth $18 Million

Bishop Jakes lives in a $1,700,000 mansion, he has been called America's best preacher and has been featured on the cover of TIME magazine. He is a writer, preacher and movie producer. Thomas Dexter "T. D." Jakes, Sr. is the bishop/chief pastor of The Potter's House, a non-denominational American mega church, with 30,000 members, located in Dallas, Texas.

9. Juanita Bynum

Net Worth $10 Million

Juanita Bynum is an American actress, singer, author, and televangelist. Her 1997 video and audiotape series, "No More Sheets", catapulted her into the spotlight in Christian circles. The reprise of the program was one of the most popular portions of the "Woman, Thou Art Loosed!" Conference in 1999, and was attended by 52,000 people. She also organized the annual "Women's Weapons of Power Conference" until 2006. She appears regularly on the Trinity Broadcasting Network, and has released a number of audiobooks and recordings of her sermons.

10. Joyce Meyer

Net Worth $8 Million

In 2005, she ranked #17 on the list of "25 Most Influential Evangelicals in America" by TIME Magazine. In 2003, she and her husband started a television ministry which

still airs today, *Enjoying Everyday Life.* Meyer only travels via private jet and responded to her critics by saying that she doesn't have to apologize to anyone about her being blessed.

11. Rev John Hagee

Net Worth $5 Million

Pastor John Hagee net worth: Pastor John Hagee is the founder and senior pastor of Cornerstone Church. He lead the Trinity Church in the early to mid-70s, and then founded his own church, The Church at Castle Hills, in 1975. Since then, he has gone on to head one of the most wide-reaching and successful Christian organizations in the world. The Cornerstone Church now has 20,000 members, and he is the CEO of John Hagee Ministries, a Christian multi-media empire, the CEO of Christian Evangelism Television, and the National Chairman of Christians United for Israel.

12. Paula White

Net Worth $5 Million

Pastor Paula White is a Christian evangelist, teacher, author, and television personality. She became a Christian in the mid-80s, and went on to launch her own church with her then husband Randy White, called Without Walls International Church. The church, which was originally known as the South Tampa Christian Church, struggled during its early years, and the Whites lived off the kindness of the congregation and the government. The church eventually grew to 20,000 members. She hosts the popular show, "Paula White Today" on the Trinity Broadcast Network, and has published ten books.

13. Bishop Eddie Long

Net Worth $5 Million

Bishop Eddie Long is the senior pastor of New Birth Missionary Baptist Church, a megachurch in DeKalb County, Georgia. When

Long started as pastor for New Birth Church in 1987, there were 300 church members, which grew to 25,000. A best-selling author, Bishop Long's captivating and powerful messages are captured in a number of books, including: *It's Your Time: Reclaim Your Territory for the Kingdom, The Elect Lady, I Don't Want Delilah, I Need You, What a Man Wants, What a Woman Needs, Called to Conquer, Gladiator: The Strength of a Man* and his most recent: *60 Seconds to Greatness: Seize the Moment and Plan for Success.*

14. Bishop Noel Jones

Net Worth $5 Million

Bishop Noel Jones earned his Ph.D from the International Circle of Faith. He then became pastor of the Bethel Temple of Longview in Texas. In the mid-90s, he became the pastor of the Greater Bethany Community Church in Los Angeles, California. When he first became pastor, the church had 1000 members. Less than ten years later, the size of the church had grown

exponentially, and the congregation had a membership of 17,000 people. An additional building was built to accommodate the number of parishioners. The church's choir, the City of Refuge Sanctuary Choir, also released a successful gospel album in 2007. The album charted on the Billboard 200, and reached #1 on the gospel charts.

15.

Minister Louis Farrakhan

Net Worth $3 Million

Louis Farrakhan reached his net worth through his leadership and brief musical career. Born Louis Eugene Walcott on May 11, 1933, Bronx, New York, he made a name for himself as the leader of the Nation of Islam (NOI) movement. Louis Farrakhan joined the organization in 1955, and he was instrumental in preserving the original teachings of the longtime NOI leader, Elijah Muhammad.

He was the man to stand behind the rebuilding of NOI, once it was disbanded by Elijah Muhammad's son, Warith Deen Muhammad, who started the orthodox Islamic group American Society of Muslims. Farrakhan restored the name Nation of Islam for the organization in 1981 and went on to regain most of the Nation of Islam's National properties like the NOI National Headquarters Mosque Maryam, as well as over 130 NOI mosques throughout America and the world. In the process, his controversial political views and outspoken rhetorical style have been either praised or widely criticized.

Black religious and social leader as he was, Farrakhan earned the tag "anti-Semite" by Southern Poverty Law Center. In October 1995, he led the Million Man March in Washington, D.C., where he called on black people to renew their vows to their families and communities. Today, Louis Farrakhan continues to be active in the NOI, but he has dramatically reduced his responsibilities due to health issues.

www.ingramcontent.com/pod-product-compliance
Lightning Source LLC
Chambersburg PA
CBHW060918040426

42445CB00011B/676